Men-at-Arms • 517

French Naval & Colonial Troops 1872–1914

René Chartrand • Illustrated by Mark Stacey

Series editor Martin Windrow

OSPREY

Bloomsbury Publishing Plc
PO Box 883, Oxford, OX1 9PL, UK
1385 Broadway, 5th Floor, New York, NY 10018, USA
E-mail: info@ospreypublishing.com
www.ospreypublishing.com

OSPREY is a trademark of Osprey Publishing Ltd

First published in Great Britain in 2018

A catalogue record for this book is available from the British Library.

ISBN: PB 978 1 4728 2 619 0; eBook 978 1 4728 2 618 3;
ePDF 978 1 4728 2 617 6; XML 978 1 4728 2 620 6

18 19 20 21 22   10 9 8 7 6 5 4 3 2 1

Editor: Martin Windrow
Index by Fionbar Lyons
Typeset by PDQ Digital Media Solutions, Bungay, UK
Printed in China through World Print Ltd

Osprey Publishing supports the Woodland Trust, the UK's leading woodland conservation charity. Between 2014 and 2018 our donations are being spent on their Centenary Woods project in the UK.

To find out more about our authors and books visit www.ospreypublishing.com. Here you will find extracts, author interviews, details of forthcoming events and the option to sign up for our newsletter.

ACKNOWLEDGMENTS

The author wishes to acknowledge the very kind assistance given by Francis Back and Yves Martin; by the Anne S. K. Brown Military Collection at Brown University in Providence, Rhode Island; the Musée des Troupes de la Marine in Fréjus, France; and the libraries of the Musée de l'Armée (Paris), the University of Ottawa, the Université de Montréal, the Canadian War Museum (Ottawa), the cities of Gatineau, Ottawa and Toronto, and the New York Public Library, as well as private collections. All this material could never have come together without the fine editorial work of Martin Windrow at Osprey. To one and all, I extend my deepest gratitude.

EDITOR'S NOTE

In Osprey's usual style, the capitalization of French unit titles, and some place names, have been anglicized in this text. Generally, French forms of place names use 'ou' where English uses 'u'. Note, however, that the French term 'Soudan', retained in this text, refers to the huge region roughly corresponding to modern Mali and part of Niger in West Africa; it should not be confused with the English and modern term 'Sudan', for the region straddling the River Nile south of Egypt, far to the east of the French 'Soudan'.

ARTIST'S NOTE

Readers may care to note that the original paintings from which the colour plates in this book were prepared are available for private sale. All reproduction copyright whatsoever is retained by the publishers. All enquiries should be addressed to:

mark@mrstacey.plus.com

The publishers regret that they can enter into no correspondence upon this matter.

OPPOSITE
Classic image of a French Navy ensign on land service overseas, *c.*1885; many naval officers were seconded as cadres to native Tirailleur units (literally meaning 'skirmisher' – light infantry). He wears a white-covered helmet; an open-collar navy-blue double-breasted *paletot* jacket with gold buttons, cuff lace and epaulette loops; white trousers, and black boots. His black belt has an oval gilt clasp bearing an anchor motif, and he wears a holster on a cross-strap for his private-purchase Leffaucheux revolver. (Print after Auguste Legras; courtesy Anne S. K. Brown Military Collection, Brown University Library, Providence RI, USA)

FRENCH NAVAL & COLONIAL TROOPS 1872–1914

INTRODUCTION:

COLONIALISM REBORN

Following the Franco-Prussian War, while a larger and far more effective Armée Metropolitaine (Home Army) was rising from the ashes of the Second Empire, the democratically elected governments of the new Third Republic had to channel the national desire for 'La Revanche' ('the revenge') on Germany while averting an all-out European war that no one really wanted. In parallel, they sought channels for promoting economic growth and national prestige. In the geo-political context of the last quarter of the 19th century, that meant taking a world-wide perspective, with the aim of securing new markets and raw materials in competition with Britain and other European powers.

Some modest colonial possessions established under the Ancien Régime had survived, and others had been added piecemeal under the Second Empire (notably in West Africa and South Vietnam) by energetic governors and Navy admirals. But it was from the 1880s that increasingly intense colonial activity was promoted by French governments as a national project, and a strong 'colonial lobby' among businessmen, politicians and the Catholic church encouraged an interest in the overseas world that – while far from universally shared – still achieved a vigour not previously seen since the reign of Louis XIV. Popular writers such as Victor Hugo and Paul Leroy-Beaulieu argued that France had an economic, intellectual, social and moral duty to colonize – indeed, the latter proclaimed that 'colonization is to France a question of life and death'. There was some persistent domestic opposition to this programme, and occasionally these far-flung adventures went sufficiently wrong to bring down governments; but, on the whole, France's new infatuation with *les colonies* would last until the mid-20th century.

In 1872, France's existing 'old' colonies were Martinique and Guadeloupe in the Caribbean and French Guiana in South America; the

By contrast, this engraving from a photograph of officers of the expedition led by Cdt Gallieni (far right) from Senegal to the Upper Niger River, 1881, illustrates the non-regulation, partly civilian dress adopted by officers in harsh field conditions; note the revolvers tucked into waist sashes.

The lethal threat from tropical fevers, and the need to carry all provisions, meant that many initial expeditions consisted of only a handful of white officers with a few dozen native Tirailleurs – rarely more than a couple of companies – with a large train of African porters. (Print after Sirouy in Gallieni's 1885 account *Mission d'exploration du Haut Niger 1879–1881*; author's photo)

tiny Saint-Pierre-et-Miquelon in North America; Senegal in West Africa; Île Ste Marie and La Réunion in the Indian Ocean; and Pondicherry with other small posts on the south-east coast of India. Recent additions were Tahiti and other Pacific islands such as New Caledonia, and, in South-East Asia, Cochinchina (southern Vietnam) and Cambodia.

An odd fact was that French-occupied Algeria, just across the Mediterranean, was not considered to be a colony at all; a legal fiction made it 'France overseas', answering to the Ministry of the Interior and sending members of parliament to Paris. Tunisia and Morocco would eventually be added as protectorates to this North African domain, whose garrisons were provided by l'Armée d'Afrique (XIX Army Corps). To most Frenchmen and their governments, the 'real' colonies were lands much farther away. Their administration was confused, involving 'turf wars' between the ministries of War, the Navy, Trade and Foreign Affairs, and an actual Colonial Ministry was only established in 1895. However, throughout the period 1872–1900, military operations in the colonies would be very largely the remit of the Troupes de la Marine (Naval Troops) administered by the Ministry of the Navy, forming a wholly separate organization from both the Metropolitan and Africa armies.

Prior to the 1880s, the Naval Troops were a largely neglected service, starved of resources in favour of the Fleet. However, when the increased tempo of operations in Vietnam and Africa began to attract more funds, officers eager for the combat experience, medals and rapid promotion that such campaigns offered increasingly applied for service in the '*marsouins*' (Naval Infantry) or '*bigors*' (Naval Artillery). From 7 July 1900, the Naval Troops became the Colonial Troops, being transferred from the Navy to the 8th Directorate of the Ministry of War, but retaining their own general staff (as well as their blue uniforms and anchor badge). When overseas, they answered to the Ministry of the Colonies.

Overseas territorial expansion

French posts on the coast of Senegal dated back to the late 17th century, but with the exception of the Lower Senegal River the interior was little-known to Europeans. It was only from the mid-1850s that the French began penetrating from Senegal towards what they later called 'Soudan' (roughly, the territories of today's Mali and Niger), which they occupied gradually during the 1880s and 1890s. Exploratory expeditions into Equatorial Africa from the later 1870s would lead to the acquisition of territories ranging from French Guinea down to the Congo River.

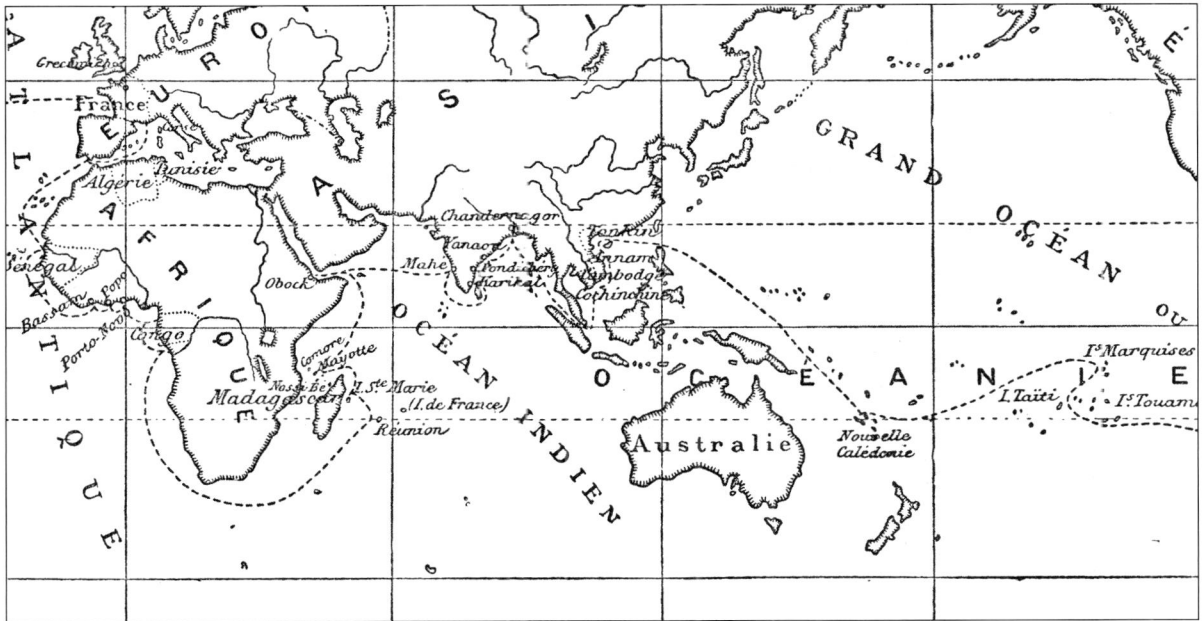

One of the great strategic objectives was to link French North Africa with the new possessions in West Africa via the huge and forbidding Sahara desert south of settled Algeria. The dream of a trans-Saharan railway came to nothing; but, after considerable efforts, three military expeditions from Algeria, Senegal and Soudan finally linked up at Kanem, east of Lake Tchad, on 28 February 1900. Native resistance collapsed in Soudan and Tchad during the years that followed, and the journey across the southern Sahara was made relatively safer by the construction of a string of forts, from which the route was patrolled by Saharan camel troops. Thus, by the first decade of the 20th century, West and Equatorial Africa were largely pacified and beginning to benefit from development of their infrastructure and economy.

The huge Indian Ocean island kingdom of Madagascar, off Africa's east coast, had long attracted French interest, and enclaves were established in the north and east at various times between 1821 and

Map embracing French overseas territories in 1887, at the time when military expeditions were securing much of West and Central Africa south of the Sahara, Vietnam and Cambodia, and would soon add Laos and Madagascar. Note the small outlying island colonies in the Indian and Pacific Oceans. (From *Les colonies françaises illustrées*, 1887; author's photo)

An image of colonial warfare as presented to the French public: an Épinal print purporting to show the action at Gbede, Dahomey, on 4 October 1892. Such illustrators did what they could, with little information and to tight deadlines. Here the Naval Infantry wear, instead of realistic khaki jackets and loose trousers, the regulation overseas field dress of white helmets, dark blue jackets, white trousers and gaiters, with red sashes. The Fon warriors are improbably armed with muskets complete with socket bayonets, and (far right) note the 'evil German instructor' – a figure of constant French paranoia at that date, as were suspected British instructors of native armies. (Private collection; author's photo)

5

1885. Tense relations with the Hova monarchy eventually brought a joint Metropolitan, Naval and North African expeditionary force under Army command in 1895, which invaded and annexed 'the Red Island' (at a shocking cost in lives to fever, which dissuaded France from ever again committing significant numbers of Metropolitan troops to tropical campaigns).

The French Navy's foothold in Cochinchina (South Vietnam) from 1859 was expanded as Cambodia became a French protectorate (1863). Annam (Central Vietnam) and Tonkin (North Vietnam) were gradually taken over during the 1870s and 1880s, in wars against both the local rulers and Imperial China. In 1887, all of Vietnam and Cambodia became 'l'Indochine française' (French Indochina), and, after a short war in 1893, Siam (Thailand) was obliged to give up Laos.

By 1886, the still expanding French overseas territories covered 3,000,000 square kilometres (1,158,000 square miles) with some 30 million inhabitants. They were thus second only to Britain's empire, if a distant second – the Union Flag then flew over 22,000,000 square kilometres (8,492,000 square miles) with 250 million inhabitants, and French territories generated 1.2 billion francs in trade compared to Britain's equivalent of 8 billion francs. By 1900, the British Empire had grown to 11,000,000 square miles with about 400 million people.

However, France's proceeds from colonial trade kept rising faster than the metropolitan gross domestic product, creating the wealth associated with 'La Belle Époque', and this was seen to justify the investment in a large colonial empire. By 1914, maps of the globe showed that territories under France's *tricolore* had grown to just over 4,000,000 square miles, though still with only some 50 million inhabitants (it was notable that the French were always far less eager to actually emigrate and settle in new possessions than were the British).

Map of West and Equatorial Africa by Capt Marceau, *c*.1911, with French territory shaded, and the names most commonly used at that time. What the French termed 'Soudan' stretched north and east of Senegal, from today's Mauritania in the north, across Mali and Niger to Tchad ('Chari'). French Guinea would occupy the gap between Portuguese Guinea and British Sierra Leone; south of 'Sikasso' (today's Burkina Fasso), the Ivory Coast would lie on the coast between US-sponsored Liberia and the British Gold Coast (Ghana). North-east of the French Congo was 'Oubanchi', today's Central African Republic. (From Marceau's *Le tirailleur soudanais*, 1911; author's photo)

CHRONOLOGY

1854 Maj Louis Faidherbe, governor of Senegal, begins penetration of interior up Senegal River.

1857 Fort built at Médina (Khasso) on new eastern border is held against attacks by army of El-Hajj Umar Tall who is building his Toucoleur empire in S. Mauritania, N. Senegal and Mali (April–July).

1860–64 Further penetrations and fort-building in southern Senegal, up Casamance River.

1859-67 In South Vietnam, French naval force captures Saigon **(February 1859)**, but is isolated; reinforcements secure city **(February 1861)**, and occupy other towns in Mekong Delta. South Vietnam is ceded to France as a protectorate by the Emperor of Annam's historical overlord, China **(5 June 1862)**, becoming French colony of Cochinchina in **1867**.

1862 France purchases territory of Obock on Somali coast at mouth of Red Sea (19 May).

1863 Cambodia becomes a French protectorate.

1864 Small African kingdom of Porto Novo on south coast of Dahomey (today's Benin) becomes French protectorate.

1873–74 French naval force invades Tonkin (North Vietnam) in December 1873, but forced to withdraw by treaty of March 1874, by which Emperor of Annam (a vassal of China) cedes some French control in central Vietnam, but not Tonkin.

1876 Guinean soldier Samory Touré establishes Wassoulou empire with capital at Bissandougou; by **1881** it will extend across Guinea and parts of Mali to Sierra Leone and Ivory Coast.

1878 Uprising by Kanak people of New Caledonia in the Pacific, a French territory since 1853 originally intended as a penal colony (June).

1879 Insurrection in New Caledonia crushed (February).

1880 Following Lt de Brazza's explorations (1875–78) and establishment of posts, the north bank of the Congo River becomes a French protectorate (September).

Tahiti and its dependencies, protectorates since 1843, become a French colony.

1880–81 Cdt Joseph Galliéni leads expedition inland between Middle Senegal and Upper Niger rivers; negotiates at Segou in Mali with Ahmadou Tall, a son of El-Hajj Umar Tall, now ruling eastern part of his father's former empire.

1881 Fouta-Djalon kingdom south-east of Senegal becomes French protectorate of Guinea.

1882 In Soudan, Samory Touré repulses first French attack at Keniera (February). In Vietnam, French naval force invades Tonkin, captures Hanoi (26 April).

1883 Reinforced Tonkin expedition captures Nam Dinh (27 March); Chinese troops and Black Flag mercenaries attack Hanoi garrison; French sortie defeated with heavy loss (14 May). Strong punitive expedition from France forces Annamese empire to accept occupation as a protectorate, including Tonkin (25 August). French face continuing resistance, but capture Black Flag base at Son Tay (15 December).

French territorial rights in Guinea are recognized. French garrison installed at Bamako, Ivory Coast (February).

1884 In Tonkin, French drive Chinese troops from Bac Ninh

(11 March) and Hung Hoa (12 April). Fighting continues; naval war breaks out between France and China (August). French force lands on Formosa, today's Taiwan (1 October). Garrison of Tuyen Quang, Tonkin, besieged by Chinese troops (12 October).

Opening of Berlin Conference to mediate 'Scramble for Africa' between France, Britain, Germany, Italy, Belgium and Portugal (December).

1885 Berlin Conference reaches main agreement (25 February): national areas of activity allocated; slavery to be abolished; rule of law, religious freedom, free trade and economic development to be established.

In Tonkin, French column takes Lang Son, driving Chinese across northern frontier (13 February); relief force marches for Tuyen Quang (16 February), breaks siege (3 March). French column crosses Chinese frontier, defeated at Bang Bo (24 March), followed by hasty retreat from Lang Son (28 March); in Paris, news causes fall of Ferry government (30 March). Franco-Chinese ceasefire agreed (4 April); by Treaty of Tientsin (11 June), China cedes Tonkin to France.

1886–88 LtCol Galliéni serves as governor of Soudan. He defeats rising (from **February 1887**) led by El-Hajj Mahmahdou Lamine. Mahmahdou forced to abandon siege of Fort Bakel on Upper Senegal River; renews attacks in Ouli province (July); defeated at Dekkele (27 October); captured (8 December), and executed. This ends resistance in eastern Senegal; but in Soudan to the east, Samory Touré can field c.30,000 infantry with modern rifles, plus 3,000 cavalry.

Comores (Comoros) Islands, north of Madagascar, become a French protectorate.

1887 Cochinchina, Annam, Tonkin and Cambodia integrated into administrative entity of French Indochina.

Promulgation of 'Code de l'indigénat' (Indigenous Code) defining status and treatment of non-European French subjects in Africa and Asia.

1891 Col Louis Archinard attacks Samory Touré's army (March).

1892 French capture Segou, expelling Ahmadou Tall. Archinard's successor, Col Humbert, captures Bissandougou, driving Samory Touré east, but Samory evades successive columns over several years.

Mixed French Navy and Africa Army force invades Fon kingdom of inland Dahomey (August), captures King Behanzin's capital Abomey (17 November); Dahomey becomes a French protectorate.

1893 *Conscription law (30 July) ends Naval Troops' annual allocation of conscripts; henceforward all enlistments to be voluntary. (This will roughly halve strength to about 10,000 men in 1897–1900.)*

Laos joins French Indochina as a protectorate following short Franco-Siamese War.

French colonies of Soudan and Ivory Coast created; Gabon becomes a French protectorate.

1895 Army-led mixed expeditionary force lands in Madagascar (March–May).

Afrique Occidentale Française (French West Africa, AOF) created as administrative entity (15 June), comprising Ivory Coast, Dahomey (today's Benin), Upper Volta (today's Burkina Fasso), Guinea, Senegal, Soudan (today's Mali), Niger and Mauritania.

Madagascar expedition finally occupies capital, Tananarive (30 September); French protectorate declared.

1896 *Costly Italian defeat by Ethiopian army at Adowa (26 March) marks virtual end of the European 'Scramble for Africa'.*

Widespread uprisings in Madagascar (April); protectorate revoked and country declared a colony (6 August), under Naval Troops Gov-Gen Galliéni. Pacification campaigns will continue until **1905**.

In Guinea, French troops end civil war at Porédaka (14 November) and annexe the territory.
1898 China cedes Guangzhou-wan enclave, on far southern coast, as a French protectorate (10 April).

Capt Marchand's 18-month exploratory expedition north-eastwards from Brazzaville in Congo reaches the White Nile (10 July) and makes camp at Fashoda. Gen Kitchener arrives up river (19 September) with strong Anglo-Egyptian force, fresh from victory over the Mahdist army at Omdurman; he rejects any French claim to territory, causing diplomatic crisis.

In Soudan, Capt Henri Gouraud finally captures the fugitive ruler Samory Touré (29 September).
1899 Pacification operations in Tchad.
1900 French military expeditions from Algeria, Senegal and Soudan meet east of Lake Tchad, establishing permanent link across Sahara desert (28 February). At Kousseri, Maj Lamy's combined force defeats army of Rabah Fadlallah of Bournou (22 April); both leaders are killed.

Troupes de la Marine are transferred to Ministère de la Guerre as the Troupes Coloniales (7 July).

Boxer Rebellion in China; French contribute to international forces that relieve siege of Beijing legations (16 August) and garrison extended enclaves.
1901 King Fodé Kaba of Casamance (area in Guinea west of southern Senegal and British Gambia) rebels against French, and executes two British officers and their escort; French column, with assistance from British Gambia volunteers and allied African warriors, storm his stronghold (May), killing him and many of his men.

Suppression of Samalat warriors in Tchad.
1902 French troops defeat Saharan Touaregs at Bir Alali (5 December), effectively ending resistance in northern Tchad.
1904–05 Uprising in southern Madagascar (November 1904), finally suppressed in September 1905.

1905 *Japan defeats Russia at Port Arthur (5 January) and in naval battle of Tsushima (27 May), beginning its rise to become the dominant military power in the Far East.*

1906 Algeciras Conference over European relations with Morocco agrees (April) to French primacy; sultan obliged to accept French financial supervision.
1907 Anti-sultan and anti-French riots (July) in Casablanca on Morocco's Atlantic coast provoke French naval bombardment and landing by troops of Africa Army (4–7 August).
1908 North African units under Gen D'Amade conduct operations in W. Morocco (January–March) in support of Sultan Abd el-Aziz; sultan abdicates (August); his successor Moulay Hafid is reluctantly obliged to accept French support, provoking continual rebellions.

Pacification operations in northern Ivory Coast, Tchad and on the Middle Congo.
1910 Afrique Équatoriale Française (French Equatorial Africa, AEF) created as an administrative entity, comprising Gabon, Congo, Oubangui-Chari (today's Centrafrique) and Tchad. Several engagements during operations to secure northern Niger, the Middle Congo and Ivory Coast.

Publication of LtCol Mangin's famous book La Force Noire, *proposing that large numbers of African troops be deployed to help repel any German invasion of France.*

French military mission (November) begins attempted reform of Sultan of Morocco's army in face of continued unrest.
1911 French troops from W. Morocco landing force – including for first time units of Colonial Infantry and Tirailleurs Sénégalais – march inland to relieve the capital, Fez, from rebel attacks (21 May). Hostile German reaction causes the 'Agadir crisis', but this is settled in November: Germany agrees to give France a free hand in Morocco, in exchange for small French Congo territories ceded to German Cameroon.

Pacification campaign in Guinea.
1912 After non-stop French operations in both W. and E. Morocco, the country is declared a French protectorate (30 March) under Gov-Gen Lyautey, soon acting in the name of the new Sultan Moulay Youssef. Operations continue unabated on both fronts **(1912–14)**; Colonial units include battalions from the 3e, 13e and 26e RICs.
1914 Germany declares war on France (3 August).

FRENCH *TROUPES DE LA MARINE &*
TROUPES COLONIALES

It should be noted that unlike the Metropolitan infantry, Naval regiments did not have a set establishment of three battalions each with four rifle companies, but might each administratively support very many companies based both in France and overseas. In 1877–78, the European establishment of the Troupes de la Marine stood as follows:

Four Naval Infantry Regiments totalling 424 officers in France, 270 overseas; 10,796 NCOs and men in France, 6,862 overseas; total, 18,352 all ranks, of whom 7,132 overseas.

One Naval Artillery Regiment of 28 companies/ batteries, plus one company of drivers, six companies of *ouvriers* (artisans) and a corps of armourers. Officers, 143 in France, 48 overseas; NCOs and men, 3,195 in France, 1,228 overseas; total, 4,614 all ranks, of whom 1,276 overseas.

There was also a 622-strong Gendarmerie Maritime serving only in the military ports of France, the Gendarmerie Coloniale, and several Compagnies Disciplinaires for convicts (see below). In all, the corps had some 22,000 French officers and men, of whom about 8,500 were posted overseas (but see note in Chronology, 1893).

Infanterie de la Marine (*Coloniale*, from 7 July 1900)

Over the following decades, the number of French-recruited '*régiments blancs*' was increased to 11 by 1889–90, these all having their depots in the main naval ports of Cherbourg, Brest, Rochefort and Toulon, plus a contingent in Paris. The total number of companies, however, remained almost the same at 178, of which 61 were at that date posted overseas. The 1er to 8e Régiments d'Infanterie de la Marine (RIM), totalling 116 companies, remained stationed in France. The higher-numbered regiments raised from March 1889, and also retitled from July 1900 as Régiments d'Infanterie Coloniale (RIC), originated in temporary *régiments* or *bataillons de marche*. These were 'task force' units, which the French often organized for particular campaigns by incorporating elements detached from permanent regiments. In the Troupes de la Marine, such 'marching' regiments and battalions were supposed to provide seasoned soldiers for campaigns and garrisons in overseas territories, where they might remain for many years (though in practice the drafts might be made up of young soldiers drawn by lot, who suffered badly from tropical climates and diseases). From 1889, they were reorganized into numbered regiments and named battalions, as follows (notes on uniforms will be found in the commentaries to Plates A & B):

9e RIM, created 1 March 1889 from Régiment de Marche du Tonkin raised in 1883, renamed 2e Régiment de Marche in 1888. Stationed in Tonkin.

Naval Infantry in France, 1876. Dark blue shako with black band, scarlet piping, brass anchor badge, tricolour cockade, and pompon in regimental colour (here yellow, for 3e RIM headquartered at Rochefort). Dark blue *tunique* with scarlet piping on collar, cuffs and front edge; two rows of seven brass buttons; scarlet anchor badge on collar; scarlet diagonal stripe of private first class on forearms, scarlet re-enlistment chevron on upper left sleeve only; yellow epaulettes. Blue-grey trousers with scarlet seam-piping, over white gaiters and black shoes. Early M1874 Gras rifle still with Chassepot bayonet; M1869 'cartridge pocket' on right front of belt.

Right: corporal wearing dark blue *képi* piped scarlet; blue-grey greatcoat, with yellow epaulettes, and double scarlet forearm stripes of rank; M1845 *giberne* on rear of belt; rectangular canteen. (Print after H. Lalisse; Yves Martin Collection & photo)

10e RIM, created 1 March 1889 from Régiment de Marche d'Annam raised in 1883, renamed 1er Régiment de Marche in 1888. Stationed in Annam.

11e RIM, created 1 March 1889 from Régiment de Marche de Cochinchine raised in 1860, numbered 3e Régiment de Marche in 1888. Stationed in Cochinchina.

12e RIM, created 10 May 1890 from six companies of 3e RIM stationed in New Caledonia in 1889. Became Bataillon d'Infanterie Coloniale de la Nouvelle-Calédonie on 17 January 1901. Stationed in New Caledonia.

12e RIC (1), created 19 September 1903. Stationed in Cochinchine. Personnel dispersed in 1907 between the 9e, 10e and 11e RICs stationed in Indochina.

12e RIC (2), created in 1907 from **18e RIC**. Stationed in Cochinchine. Incorporated in 1912 into **11e RIC**.

13e RIM, created in January 1895 from various detachments. Stationed in Madagascar and La Réunion (two companies, 1900–01). Became Bataillon de l'Emyrne in 1912.

14e RIM, created 21 January 1899 from Bataillon du Sénégal raised in 1898 and two *bataillons de marche* formed the same year. Stationed in Sénégal. Became Bataillon de l'Afrique Occidentale Française on 19 September 1903.

15e RIM, created 27 March 1900. Stationed in Madagascar, and La Réunion (one company, 1900–01). Incorporated into 13e RIC on 19 September 1903.

16e RIM, created 28 June 1900 from Régiment de Marche de Chine, which was formed with detachments drawn from Indochina. Stationed in China.

Naval infantrymen fighting in Tonkin, 1883, wearing helmet covers and clothing in lightweight black local cloth. The *kéo* blouse had a vestigial standing collar, and fastened with hooks-and-eyes or tiny buttons, sometimes with a few small 'twist' cords spaced down the front (see Plate G); the trousers were loose. For typical officers' dress, see page 41.

Here the *marsouins* have full field marching equipment, but in the sweltering climate they very often made do with a canteen and one or two *musette* haversacks stuffed with rations for up to four days. Local 'coolies' were employed to carry packs and supplies whenever possible; this was traditional in Vietnam, where the mandarins profited by hiring out peasant labour. (Print after Edouard Détaille, private collection; author's photo)

17e RIM, created 28 June 1900 with *bataillons de marche* for the China expedition. Stationed in China 1900–01, disbanded 1901.

18e RIC, created in July 1900 with *bataillons de marche* for the China expedition. Stationed in China 1900–01 and Tonkin 1901–07. Renumbered **12e RIC** in 1907.

The 19e and 20e RICs and the 1er and 3e Régiments de Garnison ('Garrison') were never formed. The 21er to 24e Régiments, the Régiment de Marche de Paris and the 2e and 4e Régiments de Garnison were stationed in France.

Bataillon du Sénégal, created 1 March 1889 with four companies from 1er RIM. Stationed in Senegal. Incorporated into 14e RIM on 21 January 1899.

Bataillon de l'Afrique Occidentale Française, created 19 September 1903. Stationed in Senegal.

Impression of Naval infantrymen of the marching battalion of 3e RIM during a surprise dawn attack on their camp at Dogba, Dahomey, on 19 September 1892. They wear white helmets and a combination of white linen fatigue blouses and trousers, with (NCO, left centre) the collarless khaki M1886 African Tirailleurs' jacket; the officer has a dark blue undress tunic laced with black. Note that the stacked rifles for which the *marsouins* are rushing are Lebel repeaters – this was the first campaign for which some French troops were issued the M1886 Lebel, though the accompanying battalions of Foreign Legion and Tirailleurs Sénégalais and Haoussas still had the single-shot Gras. (Print after Alfred Paris from field notes, *Le tour du monde*, 1894; author's photo)

Bataillon de la Martinique, created 1 March 1889 with four companies from 1er RIM. Stationed on Martinique. Incorporated into Bataillon des Antilles et de la Guyane on 19 September 1903.

Détachement de la Guadeloupe, created 1 March 1889. Stationed on Guadeloupe. Incorporated into Bataillon des Antilles et de la Guyane on 19 September 1903.

Bataillon de la Guyane, created 1 March 1889 with two companies from 1er RIM. Stationed in Guiana. Incorporated into Bataillon des Antilles et de la Guyane on 19 September 1903.

Bataillon des Antilles et de la Guyane, created 19 September 1903. Stationed in the French West Indies and Guiana.

Bataillon de la Réunion (1), created 1 March 1889 with three companies from 1er RIM. Stationed in La Réunion and Madagascar (two companies). Personnel dispersed into 13e and 15e RIMs on 27 March 1900.

Bataillon de la Réunion (2), created 23 December 1901 with two companies from 13e RIC and one from the 15e. Stationed in La Réunion. Incorporated into the Madagascar garrison in 1913.

Détachement d'Obock, created in 1888 with a detachment from 1er RIM. Stationed on the Somalian coast, disbanded in 1890.

Détachement de Diego-Suarez, created 1 March 1889 with two companies from 2e RIM. Stationed in Madagascar. Incorporated into 13e RIM in 1895.

Bataillon de Diego-Suarez, created 1 January 1905 with a battalion of 13e RIC. Stationed in Madagascar.

Bataillon de l'Emyrne, created in 1912 from 13e RIC. Stationed in Madagascar.

Bataillon de la Nouvelle-Calédonie, created 17 January 1901 from 12e RIC. Stationed in New Caledonia. Incorporated into Bataillon de Calédonie et Tahiti on 19 September 1903.

Détachement de Tahiti, created 1 March 1889 with a company from 2e RIM. Stationed in the South Pacific. Incorporated into Bataillon de Calédonie et Tahiti on 19 September 1903.

Bataillon de Calédonie et de Tahiti, created 19 September 1903 with the New Caledonia and Tahiti garrisons. Stationed in the South Pacific.

Bataillons du Maroc, created 4 August 1912. Detachments from various units used to form six mixed-race regiments, each having one battalion of European Colonial Infantry and two of Tirailleurs Sénégalais. Stationed in Morocco. Partly used to form Régiment Colonial du Maroc in 1914.

Artillerie de la Marine (Coloniale, from 7 July 1900)

The single regiment had, in 1889, 34 companies/batteries, of which 14 were posted overseas. It was reorganized on 8 July 1893 into two regiments, which provided detachments forming two tactical groups:

Gunners of the Colonial Artillery, 1906, wearing khaki-covered helmets with a brass flaming-shell badge, khaki jackets, dark blue trousers striped and piped scarlet, dark blue puttees, brown boots and leather equipment. Strangely, this watercolour by Alphonse Lalouze shows the nearest man with a scarlet collar on the 1901 khaki jacket; by regulation it should be plain khaki, with detachable dark blue patches with red edging and flaming-shell badges. (Anne S. K. Brown Military Collection, Brown University Library, Providence RI, USA; author's photo)

1st Group: batteries Nos.1 to 8 in Indochina, No. 9 in New Caledonia and a detachment in Tahiti for other Pacific garrisons.

2nd Group: six numbered batteries in Senegal, Soudan, Dahomey, Madagascar and Martinique, with detachments in La Réunion, Guadeloupe and Guiana. A Compagnie Auxiliaire des Ouvriers de l'Artillerie de la Marine was created in Senegal on 6 September 1880 with European personnel.

Uniform: In France, similar to Army artillery from 1872: dress dark blue tunic with scarlet collar and yellow flaming-shell badge, scarlet pointed cuffs and cord shoulder trefoils; three rows of brass front buttons connected with black cords; dark blue trousers with scarlet seam-piping between two scarlet stripes; shako with scarlet top and 'inverted V' side lace, scarlet falling plume and brass plate. For service with the guns they wore a *képi* and a dark blue jacket with scarlet collar patches bearing a yellow shell badge. From 1905, a single-breasted tunic had a scarlet collar bearing three-pointed dark blue patches with yellow combined shell-and-anchor badges. Officers had gold buttons, epaulettes and lace. Overseas dress was generally similar to that of the infantry except for badges, and red instead of blue lace on the 1886–95 '*cachou*' (khaki)-coloured collarless jacket (see Plate F2).

Gendarmerie Coloniale

The French Gendarmerie has long been part of the military establishment. Overseas, police and constabulary services were performed by detachments of European personnel to the Colonial Gendarmerie. In the 1870s, this had companies in Martinique, Guadeloupe, La Réunion and New Caledonia, and detachments in Guiana, Senegal, Tahiti, Cochinchina and Saint-Pierre-et-Miquelon. By 1905, the deployment was companies in Guadeloupe, La Réunion, New Caledonia and Indochina, with detachments in Martinique, Guiana and Tahiti.

Uniform: Overseas this was the same as in France, except that the dark blue tunic lacked the red plastrons; it was piped in red on the front and the pointed cuffs, with white-metal buttons, white grenade badges on the collar, white cord shoulder trefoils and an aiguillette on the right shoulder; dark sky-blue trousers with a dark blue stripe, or white trousers. No bicorne hat was worn overseas, but instead a dark blue *képi* piped in red. Both white and 1901-pattern khaki uniforms were worn overseas, with tropical helmets bearing a grenade badge. Weapons were carbines, rifles and bayonets. Native auxiliary detachments were led by French cadres; that in Madagascar had the same uniform as the Tirailleurs Malgaches (qv).

Compagnie de Discipline de la Marine

This assembled Troupes de la Marine soldiers convicted of persistent disciplinary offences. It was stationed at Saint-Pierre-et-Miquelon until

Dr Charles Hocquard, physician-major first class of the Troupes de la Marine medical staff, shown relaxing in Tonkin in 1884; in fact he was a tirelessly energetic and insatiably curious officer, who left a remarkable illustrated account of the 1883–85 campaigns against Chinese troops. He wears a simple dark blue single-breasted jacket with gold buttons and cuff lace, matching trousers and heavy riding boots, to which he would add a white helmet when on duty. (*Le tour du monde*, 1891; author's photo)

sent to the Saintes (off Guadeloupe) during 1873, and transferred to Martinique in 1890. The Corps des Disciplinaires des Colonies (Colonial Disciplinary Corps) was for convicted Metropolitan Army soldiers; from 1874, it had a company in Senegal and another on Martinique, with a detachment at Saint-Pierre-et-Miquelon; in 1891, all merged into a company at Diego Suarez on Madagascar, which had been raised since 1885.

Uniform: From January 1873, the armed cadre of officers, NCOs, corporals and drummers had the same dress as the Naval Infantry, but the only uniform headgear was the *képi*; straw hats and white trousers were worn in the tropics from 1874. The convicts had a blue (grey from the mid-1880s) *paletot* with a grey collar and cuffs and pewter buttons, grey trousers and a grey *képi*. Working dress was a linen smock, trousers and a straw hat.

UNITS RAISED OVERSEAS

The permanent units recruited in France's overseas domains in Africa and Asia (as opposed to purely local auxiliary militias) were few in the late 1870s. They consisted of Tirailleurs Sénégalais, Spahis Sénégalais and a small corps of Sepoys in India, mustering a total of about 1,500 officers and men – only about 6 per cent when compared with the 22,000 white Naval Troops. However, in the decades that followed their numbers would see a phenomenal increase, provoking strategic debates on the eve of World War I regarding their deployment. These native regulars were paid for by the Metropolitan government. In early 1914, more than 42,000 Frenchmen were serving in the Troupes Coloniales, but of these only about 13,000 were posted overseas. Meanwhile, the native regular troops raised overseas had increased from 1,500 to some 50,000 men; two-thirds of these soldiers were Africans serving in their continent, and one-third were Asians standing guard in Indochina.

In addition to these regulars on the French overseas establishment, France could call upon many additional locally-funded corps of Gardes Civiles Indigènes (Native Civil Guards); these were fully armed, equipped and uniformed, and much more akin to soldiers than to policemen except that they could not be deployed outside their respective colonies. They came under the authority of an area's senior French administrator (Résident or Commandant), and were on permanent duty, seeing some fierce battles in the course of their continuous counter-guerrilla skirmishing against bandits and local rebels. In Tonkin and Annam alone they numbered at least 8,000 men from the 1890s; counting Cochinchina, Cambodia and Laos as well, by the early 1900s French Indochina had about 12,000 auxiliary soldiers assisting its Tirailleurs and other regular garrison troops.

In Vietnam, an additional total of 4,000 uniformed and armed *Linh Co* provided a militarized constabulary under the authority of local mandarins assisting the French administration. Ideally recruited from volunteers, the men for these units could also be drafted by village chiefs to provide the desired number to be enlisted for three-year terms. They might be recalled up to five years after their service, and many made it a life-long career, retiring on a pension. Cadres were ideally six

French officers per small battalion of 345 men. Besides these Garde and *Linh Co* units, there might be other more or less permanent militias, and volunteers to support them. There were also Civil Guard units in Africa, but in lesser numbers.

Overall, the Gardes Civiles and other auxiliaries probably numbered 20,000–25,000 armed and uniformed men, bringing the total of Africans and Asians serving with, administered or supervised by the French Colonial Troops by 1914 to 70,000–75,000 – a remarkable multiplication of up to 50 times since 1872.

WESTERN & CENTRAL AFRICA

Spahis Sénégalais The need for a mounted unit in Senegal was met as early as 21 July 1845, when the 6e Escadron, 1er Régiment de Spahis Algériens was allocated to serve in Senegal, its 120 men arriving in Dakar early in 1847. All were initially Algerians, but as time passed African recruits were enlisted, and proved to be excellent soldiers when the squadron was deployed against hostile tribesmen. From May 1853 the establishment was increased to 186, with a strong French cadre of 43 troopers besides officers and NCOs, so that the squadron's actual strength soon hovered around 250. In October 1856 one of these cavalrymen, Alioune Macode Ali, became the first African Senegalese to be commissioned second lieutenant; he was awarded the Legion of Honour two years later.

During the following decades, the Spahis Sénégalais contributed detachments to many expeditions that penetrated and secured huge

The French officers in this scene of the surrender of King Behanzin of Dahomey at the outpost of Goho, 26 January 1893, exemplify the wide variety of uniform items worn on campaign, at personal taste. (Left) white service dress; (second left) black M1883 dolman, with white trousers; (third left, and far right) khaki service dress; and (second right), khaki jacket with white trousers. The gold-on-black rank lace was worn as detachable cuff rings on white and khaki jackets. (Print after Alfred Paris from photo of the event, *Le tour du monde*, 1894; author's photo)

Trooper first class, Spahis Sénégalais, c.1890 – see Plate C3. Depicted in full dress, he wears the white M1886 helmet with brass badge; a scarlet tunic with a very extended rank chevron of yellow lace; a sky-blue sash and baggy 'Turkish' trousers; and black accoutrements including a revolver holster on his left hip. (Period print, private collection; author's photo)

territories south of the Sahara; they were also deployed in Morocco from 1908. From their depot at Saint-Louis, Senegal, this elite unit also contributed cadres for cavalry formations later raised in France's vast new domains in West and Equatorial Africa. Their historian, Vaissière, records that the Spahis fought in at least 35 campaigns and battles apart from skirmishes: 'General Gallieni once said that [if they had served] in Europe, the conduct of those brave Spahis against forces so superior would have covered them with glory.' *Uniform*: see Plates C and D.

Spahis Soudanais Created on 29 August 1893, initially as a squadron of eight officers and 178 men, it had a second squadron from later that year until 25 February 1897. Its troopers, largely recruited amongst Toucouleur warriors, took part in ten major operations and several large engagements on the southern fringes of the Sahara. It was merged with the Spahis Sénégalais from 15 August 1902 as its 2nd Squadron.

Uniform: Same as the Spahis Sénégalais. While the officers do not seem to have been authorized its 1873 uniform prescribed for that unit, after the merger they were described wearing its undress. The Spahis Soudannais used the Metropolitan light cavalry M1874 saddle and later the M1885 Lefèvre, which they kept after their 1902 incorporation into the Spahis Sénégalais.

There were also at least a dozen mounted sub-units of 'Spahis Auxiliaires' attached to the regular Spahis, mostly in Soudan, though an 'Escadron de Cavalerie du Congo' was mentioned at Brazzaville, French Congo, in the 1905 Army register. These units appear to have been armed and uniformed basically like the regular Spahis.

1er Régiment de Tirailleurs Sénégalais The unit was created on 21 July 1857, as the first major step in adopting a policy of enlisting native soldiers for the garrisons of overseas territories, trained and led by Europeans of the Naval Troops. Two companies were authorized in April 1852, at Dakar and Goree; when they had proved reliable, the government ordered the organization, in 1857, of a battalion. It had six companies, at first of 86 men each but rising to 120 by 1882. By then it had a staff, a band and a small detachment posted in Gabon (until 1887). It became the Régiment de Tirailleurs Sénégalais on 31 August 1884, mustering 1,161 officers and men; augmented to 10 companies in two battalions on 11 June 1889, it raised a 3rd Bn on 26 August 1890, being numbered the 1st Regiment from 7 May 1900. The 'Senegalese Skirmishers' were in fact recruited from several different peoples of the wider region, e.g. the Yoloff of Lower Senegal, and the Bambara and Toucouleur of the Upper Niger. They served with distinguished bravery and a cheerful hardihood in all campaigns from the 1850s, and the regiment's colours, presented in September 1902, were emblazoned with commemorative honours for Soudan, Dahomey, Madagascar, Upper Volta and Ivory Coast. To these could be added Congo and Tchad (1900), Mauritania (1904–13) and Morocco (1908–13) – in all, 14 Senegalese battalions would be serving in French North Africa by the outbreak of World War I, drawn there by the widespread campaigns in Morocco. *Uniform*: see Plate E.

Tirailleurs Gabonais Originally raised in April 1883 as a platoon within the Tirailleurs Sénégalais, they were separated on 6 July 1887 as two companies, reduced to one on 25 August 1889. Stationed in Gabon, they provided the escorts for Lt de Brazza's explorations of the Upper Niger River area that became the French Congo. They were disbanded on 28 February 1891, and the Tirailleurs Sénégalais henceforth fulfilled the needs of those territories. *Uniform*: similar to Tirailleurs Sénégalais.

Tirailleurs Haoussas The Hausa are a numerous people living in today's Senegal, SE Niger, Tchad, Gabon, Ivory Coast and Nigeria. One battalion was created on 29 June 1891; it served in Dahomey during and after the 1892 expedition, and was disbanded on 13 September 1897. A Bataillon de Marche de Tirailleurs Haoussas created on 21 March 1895 served in Madagascar, forming part of the Régiment Colonial (qv), until reorganized to form the 3e Tirailleurs Sénégalais on 7 May 1900.

Uniform: The dress uniform was initially a more elaborate version of the Tirailleurs Sénégalais pattern that gradually became general issue for all African units. According to the Hausas' dress regulation of 1 September 1891, the red fez *(chéchia)* had a brass star badge; the dark blue collarless jacket had yellow edging, four yellow 'brandebourgs' of flat double lace across the chest ending in trefoils, and yellow trefoil shoulder cords; trousers were dark blue straight-cut with yellow piping, or unpiped white linen. The star badge and the 'brandebourgs' were discontinued from 18 August 1892. For undress, they were issued a collarless jacket in khaki '*cachou*' colour with yellow lace edging the neck and cuffs; a dark blue version with the same lace; linen trousers, a red waist sash and sandals. African officers had the same uniform as those of the Tirailleurs Sénégalais, who also provided the model for the uniforms worn in Madagascar by the Bataillon de Marche.

Régiment des Tirailleurs Soudanais Created on 23 April 1892 as two battalions, each of four companies, this received a 3rd Bn on 9 August 1893, and a 4th on 7 March 1894.

Tirailleur Sénégalais, *c.*1885, wearing the M1868 undress or service uniform. The four-button dark blue collarless jacket is laced with yellow at the neck and the pointed cuffs; the baggy trousers have decorative yellow knots and piping, and are confined by tall M1878 white gaiters. This Tirailleur has the single red chevron of *soldat de 1ere classe* above both cuffs, in the scooped shape termed '*en pique*', and two straight-barred red re-enlistment chevrons on the upper left sleeve only. Note that although armed with an M1874 Gras rifle, he still has the old M1866 brass-hilted '*yatagan*' bayonet. (Print after Auguste Legras; courtesy Anne S. K. Brown Military Collection, Brown University Library, Providenc RI, USA)

A soldier named Moro Diaro, 1881, when this Tirailleur Sénégalais served with the Galliéni expedition to the Upper Niger River; note his rather battered fez, and the *gris-gris* charm hanging from a bead necklace.

Apart from serving regulars, other Senegalese, often Tirailleurs veterans, were hired and equipped independently as escorts for various expeditions, which often encountered lethal opposition. For instance, Paul Crampel hired 30 soldiers for his ill-fated expedition into Central Africa in 1890-91, issuing them with red fezzes, dark blue smocks, white trousers and M1874 Gras rifles. About 70 Senegalese hired by Jean Dybowski for another attempt in October 1891 were similarly dressed, but received Kropatschek repeating rifles and accoutrements from French Navy stores. (Print after Riou from sketch by Capt Vallière; *Le tour du monde*, 1883; author's photo)

The Tirailleurs Sénégalais were not only brave and cheerful infantrymen hardened to the climate, but also versatile. This print shows some of the 150 who were trained as gunners under Naval Artillery cadres for Galliéni's column in Soudan in December 1886, when two 65mm and two 80mm mountain guns were served by mixed crews, and supported by a company of African 'artillery workers' and drivers with mules. They wear the M1868 dark blue jacket with white trousers; the European NCOs and enlisted men have single-breasted dark blue jackets, and the officer at the centre an M1883 black dolman. (Print after Riou, *Le tour du monde*, 1889; author's photo)

Serving in Soudan, Dahomey, Ivory Coast, Madagascar, Congo and Tchad, it was reorganized as the 2e Tirailleurs Sénégalais (qv) on 7 May 1900. *Uniform*: similar to the Tirailleurs Sénégalais.

Régiment de Marche de Tirailleurs Sénégalais du Dahomey Created 2 September 1893. Served in Dahomey campaign; dissolved in 1894.

2e Régiment des Tirailleurs Sénégalais Created 7 May 1900 from the Tirailleurs Soudanais (qv). Two battalions, raised to three in 1906. Served in Senegal, Soudan (1890), Dahomey (1892), Ivory Coast (1893–95), Madagascar (1895), Congo and Tchad (1900) and Morocco (1908–13). In 1908, a *méhariste* platoon of two European NCOs and 117 Africans with 120 camels was organized in its 11th Company.

3e Régiment de Tirailleurs Sénégalais Created 7 May 1900 from the Régiment Colonial de Madagascar (qv), and served in Madagascar. Formed the 4e Régiment de Tirailleurs Malgaches (qv) on 1 February 1911; a second formation of the 3e Tirailleurs Sénégalais followed in 1912, which served in the Ivory Coast and Dahomey.

Bataillon Indigène du Chari and **Bataillon Mixte du Tchad** Both created in 1900 to serve in Tchad. Formed the Régiment de Tirailleurs Sénégalais du Tchad in 1910 (qv). *Uniform*: similar to the Tirailleurs Sénégalais.

Bataillon Indigène du Congo Created 5 September 1902. Four more companies sent to form **Régiment d'Infanterie Indigène du Congo** on 6 October 1902, re-designated **Régiment de Tirailleurs Sénégalais du Congo** on 6 May 1903. Main portion stationed in Brazzaville, Congo. *Uniform*: similar to the Tirailleurs Sénégalais.

4th Régiment de Tirailleurs Sénégalais Created 1 April 1904.

Bataillon de Tirailleurs Sénégalais de Tombouctou Created in May 1906 with cadre from the 2e Tirailleurs Sénégalais; served in Soudan.

Régiment de Tirailleurs Sénégalais du Tchad Created 24 November 1910. Served in Tchad: at Ouaddaï 1909, Borkou-Ennedi 1913.

Régiment de Tirailleurs Sénégalais du Gabon Created 1 January 1912. Recruited mostly in Senegal; served in Gabon.

Conducteurs d'Artillerie Sénégalais One company of Senegalese artillery drivers created 2 August 1881, attached to Naval Artillery, gradually raised to three companies by 1914; auxiliary company created 31 January 1884. Stationed in Senegal. *Uniform*: all dark blue, red fez with blue tassel, white tropical helmet.

Compagnie de Conducteurs d'Artillerie Soudanais Created 29 August 1892. When the Tirailleurs Haoussas were raised in June 1891, two officers and 56 NCOs and men were attached to the Naval Artillery as auxiliaries; augmented by another 56 on 13 June 1893, these Hausa **Auxilaires Indigènes d'Artillerie** served in the Dahomey campaign. *Uniform*: see Plate F2.

Non-regular units:

Garde Civile Indigène du Dahomey Created 9 November 1889 as one 200-man company; received this title on 22 June 1894, and augmented to three companies, each of 115 African soldiers led by three French officers. Divided into four 'brigades' stationed at (1st) Porto Novo and Kotonou; (2nd) Wyddah and Lower Dahomey; (3rd) Grand Popo and border areas; (4th) Upper Dahomey protectorate. When enlarged to 480 NCOs and men, it was reorganized in 15 platoon-sized 'brigades'. It pacified tribal revolts, notably at Sakété in 1905 and Holli-Kétou in 1911. *Uniform*: see Plate D1.

Garde Civile Indigène de la Côte d'Ivoire Organized in the early 1900s, it took part in the pacification of the Attié area in 1909. *Uniform*: based on the Tirailleurs Sénégalais, but with six-button dark blue and khaki jackets and dark blue collar patches with letters 'GCI'; armed with M1874 Gras Gendarmerie carbine.

Gendarmes Indigènes du Sénégal Mounted squadron of armed constabulary organized from 1893–94, often taking over pacification duties from the Spahis (qv); both units are perpetuated by today's Garde Rouge in Dakar. *Uniform*: see Plate D2. There was also a group of Gendarmes Indigènes in Côte d'Ivoire in 1904; a photograph shows them wearing a fez and turban, probably a dark blue (or red) six-button jacket with the Gendarmerie's white aiguillette, and white trousers.

Engraved print from a rare group photo of West African soldiers in c.1890–92. (Left) Tirailleur Sénégalais, still wearing the pre-1889 Zouave-style bolero jacket which was preferred to the closed, four-button M1868 (see Plate E2). The other three all wear versions of the collarless M1868 dark blue jacket: (from second left to right) a Tirailleur Haoussa; a Garde Civile Indigène du Dahomey, with red lace at the neck and straight cuffs and red cotton trousers; and a Volontaire Sénégalais. (*L'Illustration,* 19 November 1892; author's photo)

A Tirailleur Sénégalais posing in field dress in the 1890s, wearing the fez with corded tassel, dark blue M1868 jacket with yellow lace trim and very baggy white trousers. The 'field' element is provided by the M1877 'coffer' cartridge boxes for his M1874 Gras rifle, *musette* haversack and 2-litre canteen. Blurred in the background are soldiers' wives, who nearly always accompanied both African and Asian troops on campaign and in post garrisons; they carried bivouac equipment and food, set up camp and generally provided assistance, which was essential to the troops' morale. (*Le tour du monde,* 1894; author's photo)

Tirailleurs Haoussas in about 1892, wearing the red fez and dark blue jackets and trousers, with a French Naval Troops sergeant on the right. (Engraving in Barbou's *Histoire de la guerre au Dahomey*, 1893; author's photo)

MADAGASCAR

Régiment Colonial de Madagascar Created in November 1894 for the 1895 campaign, with a battalion of West African Hausas, a local Bataillon Malgache and a battalion of Voluntaires de La Réunion (qv). Restructured in June 1896 with two African battalions, it formed the 3e Tirailleurs Sénégalais (qv) on 7 May 1900.

Tirailleurs Sakalaves de Madagascar This unit originated in 1869 as a recruiting company for men from the Comores Islands stationed on Nossy Bé, a small island off the north-west coast of Madagascar acquired by French settlers from La Réunion in 1840. The Sakalava were the dominant tribe of eastern Madagascar. The regular company of Tirailleurs Sakalaves de Madagascar was created on 12 August 1885; transferred to Diego Suarez, it was renamed **Tirailleurs de Diego-Suarez** on 30 May 1892 and augmented to two companies. The unit was incorporated on 13 January 1895 into the Régiment des Tirailleurs Malgaches (qv). *Uniform*: see Plate F1.

Tirailleur Sénégalais on the march with full campaign equipment, c.1900; rifles were often carried in this way. The trouser piping shows that he wears the 1868 dark blue, not the 1898 khaki uniform illustrated as Plate E3, but note the 1898 'TS' neck patch. In addition to the Lebel pouches, he has a 'de Négrier' chest rig with extra ammunition, made up at unit level. His back pack seems to be a shapeless home-made bundle, but the regulation two-part tent pole is attached to it. (Print after A. T. Goichon in *Le Passepoil*, 1922; author's photo)

1er Régiment de Tirailleurs Malgaches. Organized from 13 January 1895 as Régiment des Tirailleurs Malgaches with three battalions; the main portion was stationed at Tamatave, the French enclave on the east coast of Madagascar. Numbered 1st Regt on 6 June 1897, to have four battalions. *Uniform*: same as the Tirailleurs Sénégalais, but with red lace trim. From June 1898, red letters 'TM' on dark blue neck patches. See Plate F3.

2e Régiment de Tirailleurs Malgaches Created 6 June 1897; main portion stationed at Soamérans, Madagascar.

3e Régiment de Tirailleurs Malgaches Created 25 April 1903; main portion stationed at Cap Diégo, Madagascar.

4e Régiment de Tirailleurs Malgaches Created 1 February 1911.

INDIAN OCEAN & PACIFIC

Cipahis de l'Inde

The 'Sepoys of India', which dated back to the mid-18th century, stood guard in the small French territories on the south-east coast of India, centred on Pondicherry with secondary posts at Karikal, Yanaon, Chandernagore and Mahé. From 1867, the corps had two companies with six French officers of Naval Infantry, four Indian officers and 322 NCOs and sepoys. On 24 October 1889 it was reduced to one company whose strength, from 1891, was three French and two Indian officers, with 150 NCOs and sepoys. It increasingly assumed the character of an armed constabulary, much like the Civil Guards formed in other territories. In 1907 it was transferred to the Gendarmerie, though retaining its title, and also had a small mounted detachment. It was reintegrated into the Troupes Coloniales in 1921 and finally dissolved in 1954, when France turned over its territories to the Republic of India. Today, the Pondicherry Police wear an all-red *képi* with black piping as a salute to their predecessors.

Uniform: 'Turkish' (Zouave) style: red fez with blue cord and tassel, and white turban with red stripes; dark blue bolero jacket with scarlet lace and false pockets, small brass buttons; dark blue vest edged with scarlet; tricolour waist sash; dark blue baggy trousers for dress, white for summer. Alterations in 1884 removed the turban and added to the jacket dark blue false shoulder wings edged scarlet and scarlet pointed cuffs; a scarlet vest edged with black; scarlet baggy trousers with black piping for dress, and dark blue with a wide scarlet stripe for everyday service (see Vanson's illustration on page 22). Drummers had the same except for dark blue cuffs and tricolour lace edging the collar and cuffs.

From 1908, service dress was a red fez with blue cord and tassel, a khaki linen jacket with yellow lace edging and brass buttons, khaki baggy trousers and white gaiters, plus a white summer version. A new dress uniform appears to have been taken into wear at that time, inspired by that of the Gendarmerie Coloniale. The Pondicherry mounted detachment had, in 1910, a dark blue jacket with scarlet piping edging the collar, the front and the top of the straight cuffs, scarlet cuff flaps, brass buttons and white trefoil shoulder cords and aiguillette; blue-grey trousers with a dark blue stripe; and black boots. Initially armed with the M1866 Chassepot rifle, the sepoys received the M1874 Gras in about 1880; the mounted troopers had sabres. French officers wore their Troupes de la Marine

Member of the Garde Civile Indigène du Dahomey, 1893: red fez with yellow star-and-crescent badge; dark blue M1868 jacket with red lace trim; red trousers; and black accoutrements including what appears to be an old M1845 cartridge box at the back. Alternative baggy grey linen trousers were introduced for working dress from 1894. (Print after sketch by Gen Vanson in Depréaux, *Les uniformes ...* ; author's photo)

French sepoy of the Pondicherry garrison in India, winter service dress, 1889. This is the '*cipahis*' 1884 uniform described in the text, but the dark blue jacket and trousers have been left uncoloured in this sketch so as to show the scarlet trim clearly. (Print after sketch by Gen Vanson in Depréaux, *Les uniformes …* ; author's photo)

Comores Islands militiamen on the island of Mohélis, *c.*1900. The long smocks may be a light blue, and the sash-like diagonal ribbons blue, white and red; the long rifles with fixed bayonets may be old M1866 Chassepots. At each end of the front rank is an NCO wearing a small white turban and a white jacket with French rank insignia at the cuffs. (Author's collection)

uniforms; Indian officers had the same styles as the men, but gold-laced and embroidered.

Brigade de Garde Indigène des Somalis Created 2 June 1910. Following incidents off the lawless Somali coast, Djibouti, the main port, had been occupied by the French in 1896, with a gunboat and a small detachment of Tirailleurs Sénégalais. A local force of sorts was provided by about 140 Ethiopian and Somali *askaris* maintained by the Imperial Ethiopian Railway, plus some 80 policemen. A threat of invasion by local tribes in May 1910 spurred the raising of the Native Guard Brigade, initially 200 strong and trained by French regular cadres. Camel-mounted squads were later added for forays into the interior. The unit wore the khaki Tirailleurs Sénégalais uniform with a red fez.

Volontaires de La Réunion Originally created in July 1883 with two companies. The men of La Réunion, a small French island colony in the Indian Ocean, called Île de Bourbon in the 18th century, were renowned for their accurate shooting. These volunteer 'creole' descendants of French settlers served in Madagascar as part of the French 1883–84 expedition that occupied Diego Suarez; disbanded at the end of 1885, they wore a uniform similar to that of the Naval Infantry except for white metal buttons.

On 18 December 1894, another corps of Volontaires de La Réunion was created; by 12 February 1895 its three companies had 600 men, including 31 French cadres, with a fourth formed at Diego Suarez at the end of March. From the end of May, squads of French Naval Infantry were incorporated into the battalion. It gave a good account of itself during the advance across the island from Majunga as part of the temporarily assembled Régiment Colonial de Madagascar, whose colour it had the honour of carrying, but it remained a distinct entity. After the capitulation of Tananarive on 30 September the battalion returned to La Réunion, to be disbanded in December. *Uniform*: see Plate A2.

Milice de Comores These islands, also called the Comoros, are situated at the northern end of the Mozambique Channel between Mozambique and Madagascar. They were the site of lucrative French plantations and

became French protectorates between 1886 and 1897, usually after detachments of Troupes de la Marine and gunboats from La Réunion had restored order following internal political conflicts. The population had some Arabic blood, and islands were ruled by sultans who became subordinate to French administrators. Naval Infantry might be posted there at times; for instance, three companies were reported at Anjouan in 1886. Small militia corps numbering about 25–30 men were organized on several islands. They were issued rifles, probably old Chassepots, and achieved a certain uniformity of dress (see photograph opposite).

Tirailleurs Canaques de la Nouvelle-Calédonie A local unit, also termed 'Auxilaires Canaques' by Alfred Rambaud, are mentioned during the 1880s, probably an armed constabulary or militia raised at the time of the 1878 Kanak uprising. There were many small uprisings among this much-exploited people.

Volontaires Tahitiens One company was formed in Tahiti during 1880, and served in the Marquesas Islands.

INDOCHINA

Compagnies & Bataillon Indigène As early as February 1859, three companies of *indigènes* (natives) were recruited by the Navy in Cochinchina, some of whom were present at the capture of Saigon. French missionaries had already made significant numbers of converts, and on 19 March 1861 four Compagnies Indigènes were raised. These were organized into a battalion in February 1862, but reduced to a 235-strong company on 6 December 1863. It had a platoon of mounted guides from June 1870, which was disbanded the following year. The company was itself disbanded in April 1876, and for the next three years there were no regular Vietnamese soldiers in the French forces. *Uniform*: dark blue jacket with scarlet cuffs; dark blue or white trousers, red or blue waist sash; black turban confining the hair, under a woven *salacco* hat.

Régiment de Tirailleurs Annamites Created 2 December 1879, this unit was the tangible result of the belated realization by French authorities that if the Vietnamese were not allowed to have their own regular units to help defend their communities in a period of widespread turmoil, they might well join France's enemies. Two small 250-man battalions were later raised to three. When Tirailleurs Annamites were sent from Saigon to take part in the 1883 expedition against the Black Flag stronghold of Son Tay, the men's small stature and long hair prompted the Algerian Tirailleurs contingent to ridicule them as '*soldats-demoiselles*' (girl soldiers), but their brave conduct in the assault on the fortress earned them respect. They went on to fight courageously alongside French overseas troops in countless skirmishes against bandits and rebels, and their colour,

Map of Tonkin, Annam, Cochinchina, Cambodia and neighbouring countries in 1887, when the four regions were integrated into an administrative territory named French Indochina. The additional colony of Laos, to the south and west of Tonkin and Annam, was added in 1893 when the territory to the east of the Mekong River was ceded to France by Siam (today's Thailand). The colony's external borders were with Imperial China to the north, British-ruled Burma and independent Siam to the west. (From *Les colonies françaises illustrées*, 1887; author's photo)

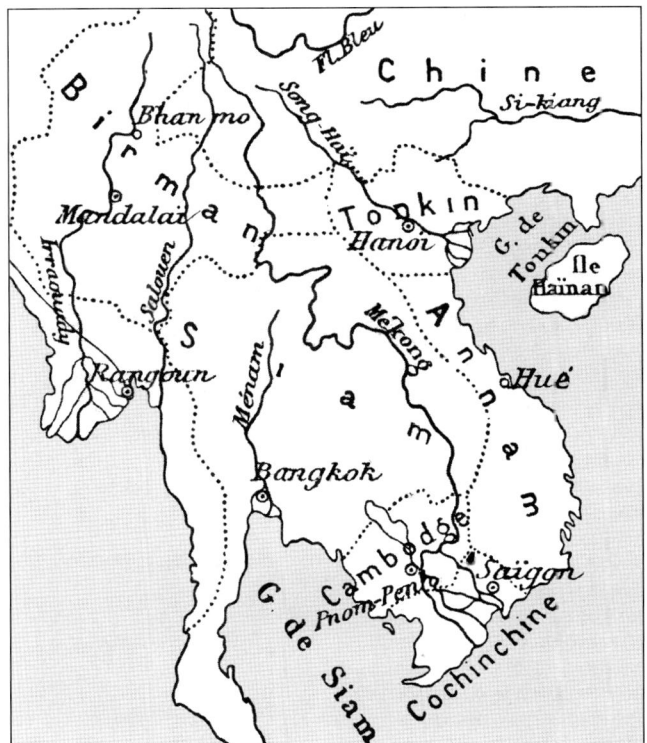

Private first class of the Régiment de Tirailleurs Annamites, service dress, c.1885; compare with Plate G3. Under the *salacco* hat of split bamboo, with a brass tip and red edging and securing ribbons, his hair is tied up with a black bandana. The uniform is all blue-black, with narrow red piping around the low standing collar, down the front edge and round the bottom, and at the top of the pointed cuffs. The small brass buttons are set on short lengths of blue-black cord. On the collar are light blue patches bearing a red company number, and above the cuffs a red rank chevron shaped '*en pique*'. A red sash is tied under the jacket, its ends hanging down at the front. Note the French Army belt buckle, and the silver 1885 French medal for service in Tonkin, on a yellow-and-green striped ribbon. (Print after Auguste Legras; courtesy Anne S. K.Brown Military Collection, Brown University Library, Providence RI, USA)

presented in 1913, bore the battle-honours Son Tay 1883, Bac Ninh 1884, Cambodia 1885 and Laos 1893–95. In spite of their services, the South Vietnamese troops suffered from slurs and discrimination from some French officials. In 1887, Cochinchina's Governor Philippi reported he did not include them in the military forces because they could not be trusted unless they were supported by European troops. They were light infantry, best employed for their agility and familiarity with the terrain; among their defenders was Gen Pannequin, who, impressed by their fighting qualities, argued for a '*Force Jaune*' to join Mangin's mooted African '*Force Noire*' in augmenting the defensive manpower available to the Metropolitan Army. Like all non-European colonial troops, their combat value depended heavily on the respect, care and example shown them by their French cadres, and they could display real devotion. Redesignated 1er Régiment de Tirailleurs Annamites on 1 June 1907. *Uniform*: see illustrations, and Plate G3.

2e Régiment de Tirailleurs Annamites Created in 1 June 1907; main portion stationed at Mytho, Cochinchina.

(continued on page 33)

TROUPES DE LA MARINE
1: Private, *Infanterie de la Marine*; full dress, Saigon, 1873–78
2: Private, *Voluntaires de la Réunion*; field dress, Madagascar, 1895
3: Private, *Infanterie de a Marine*; overseas full dress, 1890s

INFANTERIE DE LA MARINE/COLONIALE
1 & 2: *Soldat de 1ere classe*; field dress, China & Madagascar, 1895–1901
B 3: *Caporal, Infanterie Coloniale*; field dress, 1901–14

SPAHIS SÉNÉGALAIS
1: Lieutenant, full dress, 1873–1902
2: Trooper, 1873–79
3: Trooper, 1879–90

C

SÉNÉGAL & DAHOMEY
1: *Caporal, Garde Civile Indigène du Dahomey;* full dress, c.1895–1901
2: Trooper, *Gendarmes Indigènes du Sénégal, c.*1900–14
3: *Chef d'escadrons, Spahis Sénégalais*; walking-out dress, 1902–14

D

TIRAILEURS SÉNÉGALAIS
1: African officer, full dress, 1872–89
2: Private, summer service dress, c.1880–89
3: Private, field dress, 1898–1914

MADAGASCAR & WEST AFRICA
1: Private, *Tirailleurs Sakalaves*, *c.*1887–95
2: *Brigadier, Auxilaires Indigènes d'Artillerie*, *c.*1892–95
3: Private, *Tirailleurs Malgaches;* winter field dress, *c.*1898–1914

INDOCHINA
1: *Caporal-fourrier*, Matas militia; Cochinchina, 1872
2: *Soldat de 1ere classe*, *Tirailleurs Tonkinois*, 1884
3: *Clairon*, *Tirailleurs Annamites*; full dress, c.1902–14

G

INDOCHINA
1: Sergeant, *Linh Co* constabulary units, *c.*1892
2: Civil Guard, *Garde Civile Indigène de l'Annam et du Tonkin*; field dress, *c.*1900
H   3: Private, *Tirailleurs Cambodgiens*; summer full dress, *c.*1905

Musicians of the Tirailleurs Tonkinois, 1912. They wear white summer dress uniform, with red hat ribbons, red sash under the jacket and red puttees (compare with Plate G3). They display a large chevron in tricolour musicians' lace above each cuff. By contrast, the French bugle-major sergeant has a narrow band of this lace at the top of his cuffs, below gold-on-red horizontal and diagonal stripes; he also wears the yellow epaulettes of the Colonial Troops. (Print after H. Boisselier in *Le Pasepoil*, 1931; author's photo)

1er & 2e Régiments des Tirailleurs Tonkinois From the 1860s, North Vietnamese men from Tonkin often joined various French native units in Cochinchina. From 1880, ten auxiliary companies were raised, and these served well during the 1883 Son Tay campaign. At the initiative of Gen Milot, they were used to form the 1er and 2e Régiments de Tirailleurs Tonkinois on 12 May 1884. Each had three battalions (four from April 1885) of four 252-strong companies; each regiment had a cadre of 56 French officers and 174 French NCOs, and each company had 12 Vietnamese NCOs. The 1st was stationed at Hanoi, the 2nd at Sept Pagodes, both with many detachments in outlying posts.

The French press were initially dismissive and in 1884 *Le Figaro* declared that 'they cannot be counted upon' in battle, but eyewitnesses soon gave the lie to that. Companies were often co-located with French troops in small, remote posts, where their skills were certainly appreciated. They served in many campaigns and countless actions, often courageously, though their steadiness might vary depending upon both their leadership and their origins. Lowlanders from the Delta were more nervous in the jungle hills than men from highland tribes, but a British Army veteran serving in the Foreign Legion judged the best of them to be the equal of Gurkhas.

During 1888 alone, elements of the four regiments were deployed in no fewer than 54 columns that penetrated regions infested by bandits and Chinese freebooters. By 1900, Indochina had been largely pacified. Their colours presented in 1913 bore the battle honours Son Tay 1883, Bac Ninh 1884, Lang Son 1884 and Tuyen Quang 1885. *Uniform*: see Plate G2.

3e Régiment de Tirailleurs Tonkinois Created 28 July 1885 around an initial French cadre detached from the 4e RIM. Main portion stationed at Bac Ninh.

4e Régiment de Tirailleurs Tonkinois Created 19 February 1886. Unusually, this regiment came under the War Department rather than the Navy, and its cadre was drawn from the 1st Algerian Tirailleurs. It was ordered disbanded on 21 June 1890, its men being transferred to the Garde Civile Indigène de l'Annam et du Tonkin (qv). Re-raised on 1 January 1898, its main portion being stationed at Nam Dinh.

5e Régiment de Tirailleurs Tonkinois Created 5 September 1902; one company was in garrison at the French enclave of Guangzhou-wan in China. Disbanded 29 February 1908.

Tirailleurs Chinois/Tirailleurs des Frontières A company of Tirailleurs Chinois formed in northern Indochina from 4 August 1899 became a two-company battalion on 20 June 1902, and was renamed Tirailleurs des Frontières on 20 June 1905 to reflect its role as frontier guards along Tonkin's long and lawless borders with China. Although Chinese in name, its personnel were mostly drawn from anti-Chinese Vietnamese *montagnard* peoples, stationed at Moncay and Ha Coi in the border country but with a depot at Sept Pagodes in the Delta. Often engaged in border skirmishes with bandits and Chinese troops, it was disbanded in 1907, most of its men being incorporated into the 2e Tirailleurs Tonkinois. *Uniform*: Initially a dark blue Chinese-style coat edged yellow, with a yellow disk on the chest with red Chinese characters, white trousers, brown leather sandals and *salacco* hat with brass tip. Later issued with Tirailleurs Tonkinois uniforms that were not fully accepted: the *montagnard* soldiers would not wear the red sash nor shoes, found the hat unsuitable, would not cut their long pigtails, and disagreed over whether the jacket should fasten to the left or the right.

Tirailleurs Cambodgiens Created 28 May 1902, with two companies recruited amongst the Khmer population. Stationed at Phnom Penh, Kompong Chang and Pursat, Cambodia, they were mainly deployed successfully against bandits in the countryside, earning a reputation as loyal and robust soldiers, though prone to desertion. Disbanded at the end of 1907, the personnel being incorporated into the 1er Tirailleurs Annamites. *Uniform*: see Plate H1.

Bataillons de Chasseurs Annamites Four battalions each of 710 men (including 57 Europeans) were created at Annamese expense on 14 May 1886 by a French military mission sent to reorganize the ineffective Imperial army; the 4th Bn was the Annamese emperor's guard in Hué. Deployed against insurgents, they fought 'admirably well' in the 1886–87 Ba Dinh campaign and other actions. They were disbanded on 1 January 1890, the 2,450 men being transferred to the Garde Civile Indigène de l'Annam et du Tonkin (qv). *Uniform:* brownish jacket with scarlet piping and cuffs, brass buttons; *salacco* hat with brass tip; armed with M1874 Gras carbines.

Cavalerie Indigène de l'Indochine In June 1852, Adm Bonard organized a squadron of **Spahis Cochinchinois**; it was disbanded on 11 June 1871 and its horses (some imported from Egypt) were transferred to the Gendarmerie and the Artillery. In 1883, it became necessary to mount about 60 men during the campaign in Tonkin. In June of the same year, a squadron of lancers was organized in Annam and mounted on horses imported from the Philippines; they served mostly as dispatch riders, and were disbanded in 1885. Meanwhile, from May 1883, a platoon of Vietnamese **Spahis Tonkinois** with French cadres served in the field and at formal events until disbanded in late 1899. They wore largely the same uniform as the Spahis Sénégalais: an all-scarlet jacket with brass buttons, and blue bugle badges on scarlet collar patches; sky-blue breeches, scarlet leggings, and a white *salacco* edged red with a brass bugle badge and tip. The troopers rode bare-footed, since Vietnamese riders used their toes to grip the stirrups, and were armed with sabres, carbines and bamboo lances.

The Spahis had hardly been disbanded when, on 15 December 1899, a squadron of mounted **Chasseurs Annamites** was raised with 115 men detached from the Tirailleurs and led by French cavalry officers. A platoon under Lt Mussard was part of the French force deployed against the Boxers in China during 1900. This squadron was eventually disbanded at the end of 1908. Its officers wore the uniform of the Spahis Sénégalais, the men that of the Tirailleurs Annamites, armed with M1890 Berthier carbines and M1822 sabres.

Service des Remontes de l'Indochine Originating from a Metropolitan remount detachment sent to Indochina in 1886, this largely Vietnamese platoon was the only 'regular' cavalry in the peninsula between 1908 and 1914. Deployed against De Tham brigands in 1908, and also served at formal events.
Uniform: dark blue jacket with scarlet collar, grenade badge on dark blue patches, white metal buttons; dark blue trousers with scarlet stripe; white *salacco* edged blue with brass tip. Also said to wear scarlet Spahi tunics for parades.

Artillery On 12 February 1899, 14 batteries with mixed French and Vietnamese personnel were created as auxiliaries to the French regular artillery posted in Indochina. In July 1900, the 13th and 14th Mixed (Field) Batteries were in action in China supporting Japanese and Russian troops at Pei Tsang and, with the 1st Mixed (Mountain) Battery, entered Beijing in August. A squadron of Vietnamese artillery drivers had also existed since 1868; elements were attached to mobile columns sent against bandit forts.
Uniform: dark blue jacket with scarlet flaming-shell collar badges, brass buttons; dark blue trousers with double scarlet stripes; white *salacco* with red edging and brass badge and tip.

Side and rear views of a Garde Civile Indigène d'Annam et du Tonkin, c.1890, in two meticulous watercolours signed by Tran Van Minh. The hats, lacquered light brown, have bright royal-blue ribbons. The blue-black Vietnamese jackets and trousers are of the same cut as the khaki version illustrated as Plate H2, and the sash ends and puttees are the same blue as the hat ribbons. The belts, bayonet frogs and rifle slings are mid-brown leather, the haversacks light brown and the blanket-rolls dark grey. Each image shows a slightly different variant of 'de Négrier' pouch, made of beige fabric. (Courtesy Anne S. K. Brown Military Collection, Brown University Library, Providence RI, USA)

Engineers On 5 November 1904, two 124-man Annamese companies of Ouvriers-Pontonniers (pioneers and pontoon-handlers) were formed, one in Cochinchine and one in Tonkin, to perform various public works. They wore Tirailleurs Annamites uniform with a scarlet helmet-and-cuirass badge on the left sleeve.

Non-regular units

Corps de Matas As early as 1862, French administrators in Saigon recruited Cochinchinese 'Matas' or 'Mathas', who became part of a local embodied militia of about 600 men, although Capt Valmont wrote that its strength varied widely. In 1872, Dr Morice described them as being of 'Liliputian' height and 'somewhat knavish', but very good soldiers, proud of their military status and their rank badges. With other early levies they fought in several engagements, before apparently being incorporated in militia units reorganized from 1874 to 1877. *Uniform:* see Plate G1.

Garde Civile Indigène de Cochinchine Organized from 7 June 1880 by drafting 3,268 officers and men of the Milice de Cochinchine (qv), this was disbanded on 1 January 1886 and replaced by an organization made up of Tirailleur veterans who assumed many duties previously performed by the embodied militia. However, its 40-strong mounted detachment for guarding railway lines was described in 1893 as lacking military training and being armed with bamboo lances. Their old flintlocks were replaced with Berthier M1892 carbines during the later 1890s. While effective as a local armed constabulary, increased unrest in the countryside during the early 1900s led the authorities to totally reorganize the corps on 19 September 1909 into the Garde Civile de Police Locale (qv). *Uniform:* from about the 1890s, probably dark blue trimmed with sky-blue, much as the Garde Civile Indigène de l'Annam et du Tonkin (qv).

Garde Civile Indigène de l'Annam et du Tonkin Created 19 July 1888, from the Annam provincial militia organized from 6 August 1886, plus the 32-strong European police raised from 31 January 1884 in Tonkin. As the title implies, this largest GCI organization in Indochina was divided into two commands. In 1894–95, Annam had nine 'brigades' totalling 2,800 men (300-600 being detached in Laos), while Tonkin had 14 'brigades' mustering 4,000 men. Since 1892–93, Tonkin also had a special Garde Civile du Chemin de Fer (railroad guard) of 1,200 men, taking the combined total to some 8,000 men.

Uniform: European police officers of the 1884 formation wore the same as Troupes de la Marine officers, except for silver 'metal', and collars in the police's distinctive sky-blue colour (a bright royal-blue), which seems to have been inherited by the 1888 GCI. On 17 December 1887, Vietnamese *phoquan* officers were authorized probably black jackets with sky-blue cuffs and shoulder straps, silver buttons and cuff lace, with the initials of the province embroidered in silver on the collar; a black turban and trousers (or a white uniform in summer); and weapons as European NCOs. For the rankers' uniform, see illustrations and Plate H2.

Garde Civile Indigène du Cambodge This unit originated from a detachment of 50 men from the Indochinese GCI to form the personal guard of the French Resident at Phnom Penh. A royal order of the King of Cambodia formally established the local GCI on 11 July 1903, and it eventually grew to some 2,500 men. *Uniform:* dark blue jacket with small brass buttons, dark blue trousers, red puttees and red soft cap.

Garde Civile Indigène du Laos This was organized from the time of the 1893 protectorate. In May 1894, detachments of the GCI de l'Annam posted at Song-khone and Saravanc in southern Laos probably formed its cadre there. In 1899, seven brigades of the GCI du Laos existed in Upper Laos, and the service would later muster about 1,700 men. *Uniform:* dark blue jacket including buttons and cords; dark blue trousers, sky-blue puttees, black shoes; brimmed straw hat covered with sky-blue cloth and bearing French tricolour cockade.

Garde Civile de Police Locale Raised from 19 September 1909, this 700-strong unit had a cadre of an officer and 15 NCOs detached from the French Gendarmerie. Recruited amongst Tirailleurs veterans, it was armed and uniformed like the Tirailleurs Annamites, and was deployed mainly in larger towns for the pursuit of criminals, the maintenance of order, and the guarding and escort of prisoners. Like the French Gendarmerie, this rather muscular police unit was transferred to military command in wartime or other emergencies. It also had an auxiliary rural police.

Linh Co units

The *Linh Co* had long been the reserve force in all three constituent parts of the Empire of Annam (Cochinchina, Annam and Tonkin), providing a sort of sedentary militia that served only in their own province and could not be integrated into the Imperial army. When the French first took over Annam they greatly restricted the powers of the mandarins, but from 1891 Indochina's Governor-General Lanessan largely restored the authority of these local administrators. The *Linh Co* units reappeared in force, both as the mandarins' armed guards and to protect villages from the bandits and 'pirates' that bedevilled most rural areas. In an October 1891 report to Paris Lanessan stressed the importance of the *Linh Co*, which he expanded from 2,000 to 4,000 embodied villagers.

Providing an 'intimate, daily watch in the smallest villages' of the densely inhabited deltas, they assisted the Garde Civile Indigène, but were not part of it, as they remained under the orders of the mandarins rather than French officials. However, as well as hunting down local criminals and repulsing surprise attacks on villages, *Linh Co* units occasionally participated in punitive columns, and when mustered for such active service they were paid, trained, armed and clothed by the Indochina government. In April 1891, for instance, some 1,200 *Linh Co* troops with 1,000 GCI soldiers made up a mobile column under command of the local French resident and mandarins which pacified the Bay Say area. The next year, a mounted platoon is also mentioned near the Chinese border, escorting the Chinese Gen Sou to meet Gen Duchemin at Lang Son. *Uniform:* see Plate H1.

Tran Van Minh watercolour of an officer of the Garde Civile Indigène d'Annam et du Tonkin, c.1890, in white summer dress, with royal-blue sash and puttees, brown belts and holster and black slip-on shoes. The single silver cuff lace with a round 'curl' distinguishes the rank of *phoquan*. The conical woven hat is brown with a white tip and lining; the extended chin cords seem to be in green, orange and blue, since the silver flower-shaped pendant has a flat tassel in those colours. The ribbon of the bronze medal is blue, white and red. (Courtesy Anne S. K. Brown Military Collection, Brown University Library, Providence RI, USA)

Milice de Cochinchine First raised from 18 February 1862, this was made up of men drafted from local villages to a strength of two companies of embodied militia per province. They were trained by Naval Infantry cadres and, by 1877, amounted to at least 4,300 officers and men. Their roles were mainly maintenance of order, guarding military storehouses and local officials, carrying dispatches and manning riverboats. In December 1879 they numbered over 5,000, of whom 765 were drafted to form the new regular Régiment des Tirailleurs Annamites (qv). The militia was administratively abolished on 15 March 1880, but was in fact reorganized from 7 June as the Garde Civile Indigène de Cochinchine (qv).

Uniform: from 1864, a dark blue robe with cuffs in the provincial colour, white trousers and a *salacco* hat. One old M1822 flintlock musket was issued for every two men. From 22 January 1877 they were to receive a dark blue jacket, two white jackets and three pairs of white trousers, a black turban for the hair and a red ribbon for the conical hat with a brass tip. Officers designated as *phoquan* had one gold lace with a trefoil on each sleeve, and the more senior *quan* two gold laces.

WEAPONS & EQUIPMENT

Until the mid-1870s, Naval Infantry were armed with the 11mm bolt-action, single-shot M1866 Chassepot rifle taking a composite-material black-powder cartridge with a maximum range of about 1,200 yards. This was then replaced with the 11mm M1874 Gras that took a brass cartridge, with a range of about 2,000 yards; a well-trained soldier could fire some eight rounds per minute. The revolutionary 8mm M1886 Lebel rifle, with a tubular magazine holding eight rounds, naturally multiplied the theoretical rate of fire, but since the magazine had to be reloaded rather slowly with single rounds, rapid fire was discouraged except in defensive emergencies. Its main advantages were its smokeless-powder ammunition, eliminating the tell-tale white puff that located the firer, and its greatly improved range (up to 4,000 yards) and penetration. The Metropolitan Army had priority for the M1886 and improved M1886/93, so the Navy adopted instead the Austrian-designed M1878 Kropatscheck

Tirailleurs Annamites with (right) a Tirailleur Tonkinois, 1884. The shortened forearm and brass bands identify the weapon as the Gendarmerie carbine version of the 11mm bolt-action, single-shot M1874 Gras rifle, which took the old *'yatagan'* bayonet of the M1866 Chassepot. The cartridge box worn on the rear of the Army belt seems to be the obsolete M1845 *giberne*. See also page 24; the Tirailleurs Annamites wore black or very dark blue Vietnamese uniform with small brass ball buttons set on lengths of cord, a red sash worn under the jacket, and the *salacco* hat with red ribbons. For the Tonkinois, see Plate G2 and Dr Hocquard's description in the commentary. (Print after Y. Pranishnikoff, *Le tour du monde*, 1889; author's photo)

magazine rifle for its *fusilier-marins* landing-parties. However, the Naval Infantry mostly kept the Gras until they received the Lebel in 1892–94; Dahomey was its first campaign.

Non-European troops were always much slower to receive new weapons, and most kept the Gras until the turn of the century; a shorter Gendarmerie carbine version was issued to Vietnamese soldiers in recognition of their short stature (averaging about 5ft 2in). From 1902, a lengthened version of the 8mm M1890 carbine was introduced, and 24,000 examples of this 'Tirailleur Indochinois M1902 rifle' were ultimately produced. Five years later, a version extended to the same length as the Lebel rifle began to re-arm the tall African soldiers; this was termed the 'Colonial' or 'Tirailleurs Sénégalais' M1907. Both these weapons had a three-round magazine loaded from a clip, and a Lebel-style needle-bayonet. For mounted troops, see Plates C & D. Officers were armed with the Naval Infantry M1856 and 1882 swords and, usually, the 11mm M1873/74 and later 8mm M1892 six-shot revolvers.

Infantry accoutrements were of black leather, with Y-straps to support the weight of belt kit being introduced from 1893. Naval and native troops had a distinctive brass frame belt buckle, though the standard Army type with a squared brass plate was sometimes seen. The successive patterns of cartridge boxes/pouches were basically the same as the Army's from 1869 to 1914, but native troops often had obsolete patterns. African and Asian infantrymen also received a machete known as a '*coupe-coupe*'. In the field, the black tarred-canvas knapsack was very often replaced with a more practical 'horseshoe roll' made with a blanket or tent-cloth, or some other type of improvised bundle.

Two main pieces of ordnance were used by the Naval Artillery on campaign. These were the rifled, breech-loading, modified M1855 brass '4' cannon, which fired a 4kg roundshot, a 4.5kg shell or a 4.7 kg case shot out to a maximum of some 3,800 yards; and the breech-loading 80mm mountain gun ('80'), a lightened version of the army's M1877 fieldpiece, with a range of 7,000 yards-plus. The latter was first used during Galliéni's 1886–87 Soudan campaign.

SELECT BIBLIOGRAPHY

Aublet, Edouard, *La guerre au Dahomey*, Berger-Levrault, Paris (1894)

Barbou, Alfred, *Histoire de la guerre au Dahomey*, Librairie Universelle, Paris (1893)

Boisselier, Henri, watercolours of Indochinese troops, Yves Martin Collection

Darbou, René, 'Les uniformes des Troupes de la Marine et des Colonies depuis 1814', series of articles in *Le Passepoil*, 18e année to 28e année (1938–48)

Delauney & Guittard, *Historique de l'Artillerie de la Marine*, Dumoulin et Cie, Paris (1889)

Delpérier, Louis, 'Les Tirailleurs Sénégalais 1857-1914', in *Uniformes* No. 83 (Sept–Oct 1984); and 'La Coloniale 1871–1914', in *Uniformes* No. 92 (Dec 1985)

Depréaux, Albert, *Les uniformes des troupes de la Marine et des troupes coloniales et Nord-Africaines*, Ministère des Colonies, Paris (1931)

Duval, Eugène-Jean, *L'Épopée des tirailleurs sénégalais*, L'Harmattan, Paris (2005)

Francière, Eugène, 'Madagascar 1895 – Carnet d'un volontaire', ed. H. Foucque, in *Recueil de documents et travaux inédits pour servir à l'Histoire de La Réunion (ancienne Ile Bourbon)*, Archives départentales de La Réunion, Saint-Denis (1957)

Galli, H., *La guerre à Madagascar*, Garnier, Paris (1896)

Galot, A., & C. Robert, *Les uniformes de l'Armée française*, Société des collectionneurs de figurines historiques, Paris; 6 vols, n.d. (c.1957–61)

Gaulard, G., *L'Armée française*, Librairie Furne, Jouvet et Cie, Paris (1889)

Guenneguez, André & Apo, *Centennaire de la Côte d'Ivoire 1887/1888–1988 en cartes postales*, Art et Édition, Abidjan (1988)

Jolly, Laurent, *Le Tirailleur 'somali': le métier des armes instrumentalisé*, PhD thesis, Université de Pau (2013)

Historique du 2e Régiment de Tirailleurs Sénégalais 1892–1933 (L. Fournier, Paris (1934)

Lalauze, Alphonse, *Costumes Militaires de l'Armée Francaise 1902–1907*, Jules Hautecoeur, Paris (1907); numbered edition with commentaries by Louis Delpérier and added photographs, Éditions de Canonnier, Nantes (2008)

Lienhart, Constant, & René Humbert, *Les Uniformes de l'Armée française depuis 1690 jusqu'à nos jours*, Vol. 4, M. Ruhl, Leipzig (1902)

Nicolas, Victor, *Le livre d'or de l'infanterie de la Marine*, Imprimerie et Librarie Militaires, Paris (1891)

Petit, Édouard, *Organisation des colonies françaises*, Berger-Levrault, Paris (1894)

Recueil de la législation en vigueur en Annam et au Tonkin, Government of Indochina, Hanoi (1895)

Rives, Maurice, series of articles on French Indochinese units in *Bulletin de l'Association des Anciens et Amis de l'Indochine*, Nos. 1 & 4 (1993); Nos. 1, 2, 3 & 4 (1994); No. 2 (1995); No. 1 (1996); No. 4 (1997); No. 1 (2001); No. 3 (2004); No. 1 (2007); No. 1 (2008).

Rosière, Pierre, *La Garde Rouge de Dakar: Spahis et Gendarmes au Sénégal*, Éditions Les Gardes d'Honneur, Dakar (1984)

Serman, William, & Jean-Paul Bertaud, *Nouvelle Histoire Militaire de la France 1789–1919*, Fayard, Paris (1998)

Le Tour du Monde, quarterly periodical, *passim* (Paris, 1872–1894)

Vienne, Émile, *Notice sur Mayotte et les Comores*, Ministère des Colonies, Paris (1900)

Vuillemin, Henri, *La grande aventure des fusils réglementaires français 1866–1936*, Gazette des armes Hors Série No. 2; LCV Services, Paris (1996)

Weygand, Maxime, *Histoire de l'Armée française*, Flammarion, Paris (1953)

Windrow, Martin, *Our Friends Beneath the Sands: The Foreign Legion in France's Colonial Conquests 1870–1935*, Weidenfeld & Nicolson, London (2010)

A group photo of officers from Gen Dodds' mixed Army and Navy column in Dahomey, 1892. Among this motley selection of uniforms are 1883 dolmans, *paletots* and white tropical dress. The white-clad officer behind the left-hand seated figure seems to have long horizontal grenade badges on his collar and that of the Naval Artillery on his helmet; these identify him as from the expedition's Foreign Legion battalion. At this date, Naval Infantry officers wore regimental numbers on their caps and collars. (*Le tour du monde*, 1894; author's photo)

PLATE COMMENTARIES

UNIFORMS & EQUIPMENT

A: *TROUPES DE LA MARINE*

The uniforms of the European personnel can be divided between what was worn in France and what was worn overseas; these Plates are devoted to the latter only.

In France, from 18 January 1873, the men's dress uniform consisted of a frock-like dark blue double-breasted *tunique* with two rows of seven brass buttons; scarlet fouled-anchor

Two Naval Troops engineer officers in Tonkin, 1884–86. Although engineers detached from the Metropolitan Army had historically served in overseas territories, a lack of willing candidates in the 1870s led to an order of 26 June 1880 giving the Naval Artillery responsibility for all military constructions and fortifications overseas (although Metropolitan engineer detachments continued to be posted to Indochina and West Africa for major projects such as railway construction). Both officers wear black-covered helmets with a gilt badge combining the Engineers' helmet-and-cuirass with the Navy's anchor. The lieutenant (left) has a dark blue *paletot* with gold lace cuff rings, epaulette loops and Artillery flaming-shell collar badges; his dark blue trousers have scarlet seam-piping between double stripes. The captain (right) wears a black Vietnamese very low-collared *kéo* jacket and trousers, with added gold lace, and three rows of small buttons set on four transverse cords. (Print after J. E. Hilpert from photos; private collection, author's photo)

badges sewn both inside and outside the collar, so as to show when this was worn either open or closed; scarlet piping; yellow epaulettes; blue-grey trousers and a dark blue shako, both with scarlet piping, the latter with a pompon in company colour (1st scarlet, 2nd yellow, 3rd green, and white for unattached men), and a brass anchor plate.

For undress, a dark blue *képi* with scarlet piping and scarlet anchor badge was worn, and a dark blue double-breasted *paletot* (basically a short-skirted, unpiped version of the *tunique*), with two rows of five buttons, dark blue epaulette-retaining loops piped red, and red anchor badges on a standing collar. The dress shako was replaced from 1885 with a stiffened dress *képi* with a pompon. On 21 October 1886, the *tunique* was abolished in favour of the *paletot,* with yellow epaulettes for formal orders of dress. The *képi* and collar anchors were replaced with red regimental numbers from 2 May 1890; these changed to brass from December 1894; to brass anchors from June 1904; and to a regimental number on the collar and an anchor on the *képi* from 20 July 1909.

In the colonies, application of these regulations was sometimes anticipated (e.g. abandonment of the *tunique*) and sometimes considerably delayed (e.g. introduction of collar numbers). As partly illustrated in Plates A & B, overseas dress was of a bewildering variety; for instance, in Vietnam local woven hats and black or dark blue *kéo* jackets and trousers were used in the field during the 1880s. (Note that while the plate-like Annamese *salacco* hat was originally particular to Central and South Vietnam, it was later extended to some North Vietnamese units; and note particularly that during the 1880s 'salacco' became a slang term not only for all Indochinese headgear, but also for the French tropical helmet, so period accounts should be read with caution.)

Officers in France had an 1873 uniform basically similar to that of their men, but with dark blue trousers and gold buttons, anchor badges, epaulettes and lace. In 1883, their uniform changed to a black single-breasted hussar-style dolman or 'attila' with black braid and trefoil chest-cords, gold cord trefoil shoulder-knots and 'Austrian knot' rank lace on the sleeves; their grey-blue trousers had a dark blue stripe, and their *képi* gold piping. In 1893, the dolman was replaced with a single-breasted dark blue tunic with three-button cuff flaps, cuff-rings of gold rank lace, gold buttons, collar and cap badges, and epaulettes for formal orders of dress. Overseas, elements of the 1873, 1883 and 1893 uniforms might be seen worn mixed with hot-weather items in white or light khaki, or even with civilian garments, according to personal or unit preference.

A1: Private, *Infanterie de la Marine*; full dress, Saigon, 1873–78

During the 1860s and 1870s the French authorities in Cochinchina made concessions to the intense heat and humidity of the climate by allowing the use of local bamboo, straw or reed woven hats, usually with a white linen cover, and open collars. This soldier wears the dark blue frock-tunic that was regulation in the colonies until 31 March 1878, piped scarlet and with scarlet anchor badges on the inside of the opened collar; yellow fringed epaulettes were added for formal orders of dress. The white linen trousers are confined by M1855/67 nine-button gaiters. The rifle is the M1966 Chassepot, and he has an M1869 'cartridge pocket' on his belt.

A2: Private, *Volontaires de La Réunion*; field dress, Madagascar, 1895

From December 1894, this unit was issued the same colonial uniform as the Naval Infantry regiments. By 16 March, volunteer Eugène Francière mentioned his shined shoes, his gaiters, his shiny buttons and belt buckle, his white helmet (see A3), and the bayonet to fit on his Lebel rifle, all of which testifies that supplies had arrived. A blurry photo shows the battalion parading in white tropical dress with helmets when leaving La Réunion. In Madagascar, they further received the light khaki ('cashew-colour') Naval Troops uniform introduced on 21 October 1886. The collarless, four-button jacket was that of the African Tirailleurs (see Plate E3); it was trimmed

Private of the 18e RIM in northern China, winter 1900–01. To protect against the freezing weather, the *marsouins* who remained in garrison after driving the Boxers from Beijing were issued grey-blue Chasseurs Alpin capes and dark blue berets (with a red anchor badge added), as well as greatcoats, puttees, sheepskin jerkins, mittens or gloves, worn with scarves and warmer boots. (Print after Henri Boisselier from period descriptions; private collection, author's photo)

with lace (tape edging) at neck and cuffs in dark blue for infantry and red for artillery. Francière further noted on 3 April 1895 that the volunteers 'gave a reddish hue' to their hitherto white helmets (presumably using the mud of the 'Red Island'), put some earth into their bayonet scabbards to suppress rattling and covered them with rags to prevent glinting reflections. Note that this man has a single M1877 cartridge pouch; he also wears slung the standard-issue two-spout canteen and *musette* haversack.

On 31 May, in accordance with contemporary beliefs about avoiding fevers (which killed some 30 per cent of the expeditionary force), the battalion were ordered to wear after sunset the dark blue Naval Infantry *paletot* tunic, a waist sash (presumably red) and dark blue Chasseurs Alpin-pattern berets bearing a red anchor badge. The helmet was otherwise always worn.

A3: Private, *Infanterie de la Marine*; overseas full dress, 1890s

In the colonies, the *paletot* was worn for this order of dress from 1878 until 1901, with yellow epaulettes, and unconfined white trousers. Photographs suggest that the red anchor collar badge was not replaced by regimental numbers in the colonies until about 1895. Blue-grey trousers with red seam-piping were regulation winter wear in 1881–91, but were little used in the tropics. Headdress in most colonies consisted of a local woven straw, bamboo or reed hat covered with white linen, until the introduction of a white-surfaced cork tropical helmet from 31 March 1878. This had an outswept rear neckguard; its replacement from 21 October 1886 had a more vertical profile at the back and thus a more down-curved lower edge, and also introduced a pin-on brass anchor badge on the front. For formal summer dress, the dark blue *paletot* was replaced with a white version from 8 February 1895, with a stand collar, open patch skirt pockets and five or six front buttons; this was worn with dark blue collar patches edged with scarlet and bearing a scarlet anchor, as Plate B3. In torrid Indochina, the dark blue *paletot* was officially replaced by the white uniform for all-year-round formal dress from 1901, but the 9e RIC in Hanoi were still seen in the *paletot* and blue-grey trousers after that date. This *marsouin* parades with Lebel rifle pouches supported by the M1892 Y-straps, and note also that he carries a canteen even with dress uniform. His 1893 Colonial Medal bears a campaign clasp.

B: *INFANTERIE DE LA MARINE/COLONIALE*

B1 & B2: *Soldat de 1ere classe*; field dress, Madagascar & China, 1895–1901

These figures are reconstructed from well-known photographs taken in Hanoi by Vu Chong, and are presumed to show a *marsouin* equipped for the 1900 expedition to Beijing.

This field dress introduced from 8 February 1895 was made of cloth in a shade called *bleu mécanicien* (mechanic's blue) – a medium blue-grey somewhat reminiscent of today's blue denim material – which was unpopular with the authorities because it quickly discoloured with wear and washing. It was used for a helmet cover, a five-button jacket with a stand collar and trousers, which were worn by Naval Infantry both in Madagascar and China; this 'private first class' has his single red rank stripe buttoned to each forearm.

Good service in the coming campaign may bring him the second stripe of *caporal,* with slightly higher pay and an easier life in barracks. Enlisted men's stripes were set diagonally above the cuffs for infantry and certain other foot troops, or as points-up chevrons for Chasseurs, cavalry, artillery and certain other corps – including native Tirailleurs. They were of textured red woollen braid, and those of sergeants and above of textured bullion braid in gold or silver according to the branch's 'metal' – its button colour – on red backing that showed slightly at the long edges. Early in the 20th century the former re-enlistment chevrons, worn in red on the upper left sleeve, were replaced with a line of piping around the top of the cuff, in red or button-colour for troops or NCOs.

The long white canvas gaiters may be either the M1874 with 15 bone buttons, or the 12-button M1894. Over the belt and Y-straps that support his Lebel rifle equipment, he has a blanket roll to which his red-piped dark blue *kepi* is attached by its chinstrap and his messtin by its handle. His tin *quart* mug hangs from the sling of the M1877 2-litre, two-spout canteen, which is covered with old dark blue uniform cloth; this balances the weight of his khaki M1892 haversack, hanging over his bayonet on the left.

B3: *Caporal, Infanterie Coloniale*; field dress, 1901–14
On 3 June 1901 a new light khaki service and field uniform was introduced; it too included a cover for the M1886 helmet, not illustrated here. The six-button jacket had shoulder straps, interior breast pockets and flapped skirt pockets. The stand collar bore dark blue patches on red backing bearing red anchor badges, and rank stripes were buttoned to the sleeves. Even assuming his luck and health hold up, this corporal may wait years for the next step. The gulf between corporal and sergeant was considerable in the French armed services: the one belonged to the '*troupes*', the other to the much more highly paid '*sous-officiers*'.

Unlike the collarless M1886 Tirailleurs' pattern (see A2), the *marsouins* judged the 1901 khaki uniform to be a success, and from 1909 it became the confirmed issue for all overseas troops, though in practice it appeared in many combinations during colonial service. We illustrate the regulation belt pouches for the Lebel rifle, but in the colonies both *les colonials blancs* and native Tirailleurs made frequent use of variations on the extra home-made horizontal chest pouches that are often called 'de Négrier', after the Foreign Legion colonel who ordered his men to make them up in scrap uniform cloth or leather. In the 1890s they were often divided in two sections and worn slung under the arms from shoulder straps crossing on the back.

C: *SPAHIS SÉNÉGALAIS*
C1: Lieutenant, full dress, 1873–1902
The distinctive regimental colours illustrated were those of the parent unit, the 1er Régiment de Spahis Algériens. Initially the all-French officers seem to have preferred to keep their old regiment's 'Turkish' style full dress, or simple Troupes de la Marine dark blue or white tunics. Some acquired a scarlet dolman with sky-blue cuffs, black lace and cording and gold sleeve-knots, worn with sky-blue trousers with scarlet stripes, and a completely sky-blue *kepi* with gold lace according to rank. From 1873, the regulation officers' dress uniform was this Chasseurs à Cheval pattern, with the trefoil shoulder cords in black or gold according to order of dress, and gold star-over-crescent *kepi* and collar badges. The scarlet trousers with two sky-blue stripes and seam-piping were tailored fuller to be worn with black shoes when on foot, and as breeches to be worn with riding boots, as here. He carries the officers' version of the M1822 light cavalry sabre.

This uniform was not especially practical for campaign or even service dress in the gruelling conditions of West and Equatorial Africa. We have only seen one Épinal image printed in France showing a Spahis officer wearing the 1873 uniform, leading a cavalry charge during the advance on Kana, Dahomey, in November 1892, and he also wears the white helmet and a red waist sash. Many officers procured more suitable scarlet jackets resembling the men's 1873 pattern (see C3); this seems to have become a semi-official field dress, worn with sky-blue, red, grey or white trousers, white helmet with badge or the M1873 *kepi*. Another Épinal print depicting the entry into Timbuktu on 10 January 1894 shows all Spahis, African or French, wearing the same dress: white helmets, red jackets, sky-blue trousers with red stripes and red waist sashes; only the trumpeters have reversed colours. Several officers' photographs of the 1890s show this do man with gilt star-and-crescent badges on sky-blue collar patches, and pocket slits in the breast.

C2: Trooper, 1873–79
The troopers' original uniform, worn until 1879, was that of the 1858 regulations for the 1er Spahis Algériens, in all its Arabic splendour. The scarlet bolero-type jacket has the unit's

Kettledrummer of the Spahis Sénégalais, 1913. This veteran of at least two campaigns wears the same basic uniform as Plate C3, with the yellow chevron of a *soldat de 1ere classe* above both cuffs and two sky-blue re-enlistment chevrons on his left upper sleeve. The saddle blanket is red, the drums red with yellow decorations. Just visible here is the brown waist belt incorporating small pouches for the M1890 Berthier carbine's three-round clips. (Print after H. Feist in *Le Passepoil*, 1928; Yves Martin Collection, author's photo)

sky-blue *tombeau* patches and shallow triangular cuff facings with black lace edging, worn over a sky-blue vest, both decorated with black cord and tracery. Below the broad crimson sash are very full sky-blue 'Turkish' trousers. Over all is worn a flowing white *bournous*, initially wool but later cotton; a second, longer, hooded cloak in scarlet, partly lined in white, is worn over this against the cold of night. The two layers are bundled together at the upper chest and the hood thrown right back, obscuring the outer garment's small sky-blue chest fastenings and the black lace edging to the hood. (Trumpeters wore reversed colours: sky-blue jacket and vest trimmed with yellow, scarlet trousers with yellow lace, and sky-blue hooded cloak lined white and with scarlet lace edging.) Initally the headdress was the red *chéchia* fez with a sky-blue cord and tassel, wrapped in a white turban with blue lines. In 1862–63, wide-brimmed straw hats were issued as protection from the sun, but from 1873–74 a white helmet was adopted. This became regulation (alongside the *chéchia*) in 1878, with a brass star-and-crescent badge. Initially troopers wore Arab boots, but later they received those used by the French cadres; our figure thus represents *c*.1878–79.

His weapons are the M1822 sabre and a slung Chassepot M1866/69 rifle 'for African cavalry'. From about 1850, the Spahis Sénégalais also had a platoon armed with M1823 lances of blackened ash with steel spearheads and heels. They were successfully used in combat and, in 1862, a second lancer platoon was formed. In 1872, lances were abolished in the Metropolitan cavalry and so went out of use in West Africa about three years later. The pennant was originally blue, white and red, but later white and red only.

C3: Trooper, 1879–90

From 1879, the 'Turkish'-style bolero and vest were replaced with a simpler style. An all-scarlet, single-breasted, five-button jacket had yellow pointed lace at the cuffs, and small three-pointed scarlet collar patches bearing the star-and-crescent badge; a scarlet waist sash was worn over plain sky-blue baggy trousers, and the black cavalry boots had steel spurs. The white, brass-badged M1878 helmet was later replaced with the M1886 pattern. The fez also received the badge early in the 20th century. Trumpeters had a sky-blue jacket with red trousers until 1900, when they changed to the standard uniform with the addition of tricolour lace at the collar and cuffs (see Plate G3). No other basic changes were made before 1914. A summer jacket was white, with two breast pocket flaps (without buttons), the rest of the uniform being unchanged. The Spahis were not issued khaki uniforms.

Armament consisted of the M1822 and later M1822/80 light cavalry sabre in the troopers' and officers' versions, with a brass guard and steel scabbard. The troopers' M1873 and officers' M1874 revolvers were later replaced for all ranks with the M1892; holsters were slung on the left side. The troopers also carried, successively, the Chassepot M1866/69 rifle for the North African cavalry, the Gras M1874, and the Berthier M1890 and M1892 cavalry carbines. The accoutrements were all of blackened leather until 1900, when the diagonal pouch belt over the left shoulder was replaced with a reddish-brown waist belt incorporating small pouches holding the three-round stripper clips for the M1890 carbine; the other belts and holsters remained black.

The saddles were of the same Arab type as used by Algerian Spahis, of red-brown leather, featuring a seat that almost enclosed the rider and large 'shoe' stirrups. Large brown canvas and leather saddle bags hung on each side at the cantle, over a spare horseshoe case on the left and below the rolled and strapped *bournous* cloak when it was not being worn. The sabre was thrust under the left flap of the saddle. Rifles were usually worn slung round the body, but the high cantle sometimes made this awkward, so troopers resorted to slinging them to the front right of the saddle.

D: DAHOMEY & SÉNÉGAL

D1: *Caporal, Garde Civile Indigène du Dahomey*; full dress, *c*.1895–1901

From 1889, full dress consisted of a Zouave-pattern dark blue jacket and vest with red lace and piping, medium blue waist sash, plain red baggy trousers, bare lower legs and white or tan slipper-like shoes, and a red fez with blue cord and tassel and brass star-and-crescent badge. (Note that photographs of all African troops show a wide range of shapes for the fez, including this 'flowerpot' profile.) From June 1894, the trim on the full dress bolero jacket and vest changed to green, as worn by this corporal. Service dress consisted of the dark blue collarless M1868 *paletot* with baggy grey linen trousers. The weapon was the M1874 Gras, presumably with the M1877 cartridge box worn centrally at the rear of the belt. French officers had an all-dark blue dolman without cords, with star-and-crescent collar badges, seven gilt front buttons and gold epaulette loops; infantry trousers (*garance* red with a black stripe); and a Gendarmerie-pattern dark blue *képi* with gold lace and star-and-crescent badge. A white helmet and uniform were worn in the field. The enlisted ranks' uniform was changed from 22 June 1901 to a dark blue dress jacket with green cuffs and lace and four white metal buttons,

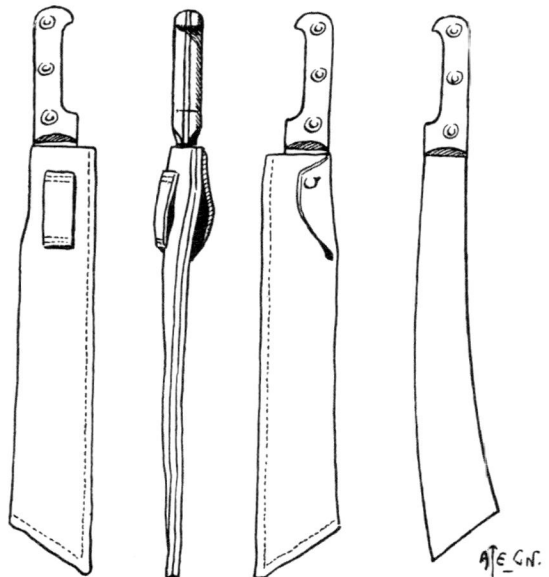

Drawings of the issue *coupe-coupe* machete and its leather scabbard, as added to the belt kit of many African and Indochinese Tirailleurs in *c*.1880–1914. It was a necessary tool for hacking paths through thick vegetation for the troops and their often lengthy columns of local porters. (Print after A. T. Goichon in *Le Passepoil*, 1922; author's photo)

cut as Plate F3, or a plain dark blue field version, with blue linen trousers; the fez was unchanged.

D2: Trooper, *Gendarmes Indigènes du Sénégal, c.*1900–14
A decree of 29 December 1894 states that the Gendarmes Indigènes, organized from 1893–94, had a uniform in the Algerian Arab style somewhat like the Spahis Sénégalais' pre-1879 uniform. Troopers had a blue-tasseled red fez wrapped in a white turban; a scarlet jacket with sky-blue cuffs and edging and black lace and tracery, over a sky-blue vest with black trim; a sky-blue waist sash; plain dark blue baggy trousers; initially these tan-brown Arab boots, and later black French spurred boots. The inner cloak was white, under the sky-blue hooded one worn here. The Gendarmes Indigènes had the same weapons as the Spahis (Plate C), but used the Metropolitan M1874 light cavalry saddle.

D3: *Chef d'escadrons, Spahis Sénégalais*; walking-out dress, 1902–14
This officer with the cavalry rank equivalent to major is based partly on a *c.* 1905 photograph of Justin Nicolas René Potvin (1858–1930). Born in Gorée, he was one of the first officers of African blood in the Spahis Sénégalais, becoming a lieutenant in 1895 at the age of 36, captain in 1902, and commander of 1st Sqn in 1905. He was later awarded the Legion of Honour for his services. The officers' dress uniform changed in 1902 from that illustrated as Plate C1 to this all-scarlet nine-button tunic, the cuffs now having a three-button flap and rings of flat gold rank lace. Gold-fringed epaulettes were worn with full dress, here with the short, thick fringes of field-grade officers. Another change was the entirely sky-blue *képi* with gold rank lace and badge. The star-and-crescent also appeared on the stand collar and on the white helmet. The latter, with a red-lined white cloak, was often worn for parades.

E: *TIRAILLEURS SÉNÉGALAIS*
E1: African officer, full dress, 1872–89
French officers and senior NCOs serving in the Tirailleurs Sénégalais wore the uniform of the Naval Infantry African officers had the same dark blue Zouave 1857 pattern uniform as their men, but richly laced and embroidered with gold, and with a scarlet waist sash, black boots and (according to prints) a gold cord and tassel to the red fez. From 11 June 1889 the African officers' dress uniform was altered: the gold-laced bolero jacket became sky-blue, worn over a similarly decorated sky-blue vest (called a *sédria*), with sky-blue baggy trousers with a yellow stripe, and black boots. Field dress was an unlaced sky-blue bolero and vest with sky-blue or white trousers, lace-up boots and white helmet. From 18 June 1898, this changed to a dark blue dolman with flat black lace, yellow-piped dark blue trousers, laced short boots and the fez or white helmet. Although not found in regulations, the French Colonial Infantry officers' jacket was often seen worn by African officers from the early 1900s. Tirailleurs officers did not have specific regulation swords, but generally favoured the Chasseur model and, eventually, the M1882 infantry sword; both patterns had steel hilts. (Plate after Legras; *Le Petit Journal*, 7 March 1891)

E2: Private, summer service dress, *c.*1880–89
The 1857 decree specified a dark blue Zouave-style uniform: a 'Turkish' bolero jacket edged with yellow lace and piping over a yellow-edged *sédria*, a red waist sash, yellow-piped baggy trousers as well as this pair made of plain white linen, and short white gaiters with yellow-tan leather *jambières* upper leggings recalling the Metropolitan infantry's 1860

regulations. The red fez had a medium-blue cord and tassel and a white turban, and they received a Zouave-pattern greatcoat. On 18 February 1868, a dark blue four-button collarless jacket (officially called a '*paletot*', though it in no way resembled the European troops' tunic), edged with yellow lace at the neck and pointed cuffs, was introduced as field dress – i.e. a decorated dark blue version of figure E3's khaki jacket (see illustration on page 17). In 1873, it was ordered that this should replace the Zouave-style service dress uniform, with straight-cut trousers and no turban, but this was so much resented by the Tirailleurs that this original Zouave style was restored in 1876, with tall white gaiters from 1878. Sandals could be worn with field dress from 1881, with a small strap linking them with the gaiter's lower button. The Tirailleurs Sénégalais were initially armed with M1840 Navy double-barrelled rifles, which were replaced with the M1874 Gras in about 1880. (Valmont Ms, Bibliothèque Nationale, Paris)

E3: Private, field dress, 1898–1914
On 11 June 1889 the Zouave-pattern uniform was finally abolished for enlisted men. Instead, for dress uniform they wore the red fez with blue cord and tassel but without a turban; the M1868 collarless, closed, four-button dark blue jacket with yellow lace at neck and cuffs; a red waist sash; dark blue baggy trousers with yellow piping, or white summer trousers; white gaiters, and shoes. For undress and campaigns they might wear (though not invariably) this light khaki linen version, with khaki linen gaiters. From 18 June 1898, all African Tirailleurs units were to display at the jacket neck, for all orders of dress, detachable dark blue rectangular patches bearing in red letters 'TS' (Tirailleurs Sénégalais), 'TM' (Tirailleurs Malgaches) or 'TH' (Tirailleurs Haoussas). The trousers assumed this straighter, tapered *culotte* shape, and khaki puttees were issued, as well as this undress fez without a tassel. Footwear was initially sandals, although Army shoes were increasingly seen after 1900. This 1898 order of dress remained unchanged until 25 June 1914. The Lebel rifle equipment was worn with the addition of a *coupe-coupe* in a leather sheath at right rear. Note too the bundled cloth *barda* (Army slang for a pack) tied on around the shoulders with twisted cloth, often used in preference to a knapsack.

F: MADAGSCAR & WEST AFRICA
F1: Private, *Tirailleurs Sakalaves, c.*1887–95
The unit's first uniform in 1885 was a dark blue single-breasted jacket with red collar, red-piped front edge and red pointed cuffs, brass buttons, white straight trousers and red fez with blue tassel. This was changed in about 1887 to this more European-style tunic, with a red collar, straight cuffs and shoulder straps, blue or white trousers according to season, and a dark blue pillbox-like round cap with a red band bearing a blue anchor badge. The collar had dark blue patches with an 'S' cut out of red cloth. During the Madagascar campaign in March 1895, Volontaires de La Réunion soldier Eugène Francière saw Tirailleurs Sakalaves wearing 'an attractive and original uniform: blue linen blouse with red cuffs and shoulder straps, short and baggy grey or white trousers, fez garnished by its wearer with a superb red or blue pompon.' By that time the unit had been ordered merged into the Régiment des Tirailleurs Malgaches since 13 January 1895, but in practice any change of dress would have taken some time, especially under campaign conditions. (General Vanson's notes, 1889, Musée de l'Armée, Paris)

F2: *Brigadier, Auxiliaires Indigènes d'Artillerie*, c.1892–95

According to General Vanson's notes of 1893, Hausa auxiliary gunners attached to the regular Naval Artillery wore an M1889 'cashew'-khaki collarless jacket similar to that of the African Tirailleurs but trimmed at neck and pointed cuffs with red rather than yellow, with brass buttons, tan linen trousers and the blue-tasselled red fez; this man, practising gun drill with an unfuzed 80mm shell, sports the two red chevrons of corporal's rank. A surviving c.1905–10 uniform is of the 1889 pattern all in dark blue, with the same red lace at neck and cuffs, and dark blue detachable neck patches bearing a red flaming-shell badge.

F3: Private, *Tirailleurs Malgaches*; winter field dress, c.1898–1914

When formed from 1895, the regiment was assigned the 1889 regulation Tirailleurs Sénégalais uniforms by then common to

Detail from a print after Alfred Paris, drawn from sketches and descriptions of the proclamation of Behanzin's pliable successor as King of Dahomey on 15 January 1893. It shows Tirailleurs Sénégalais wearing a mixture of khaki jackets and white fatigue smocks, all with white trousers and barefoot. As in so many African campaigns, the Tirailleurs' relatively greater resistance to disease made them an absolutely necessary component of any column, but they still suffered significant losses. (*Le tour du monde*, 1894; author's photo)

all African foot troops; from June 1898, they received dark blue neck patches with red cut-out letters 'TM'. The dark blue jacket and trousers with yellow lace and piping respectively were worn for everyday service and formal dress, but also on campaign, sometimes with khaki trousers and puttees, or white trousers issued for hot weather. Here we show the trousers worn untied, over what seem from photographs to be long woollen drawers. This soldier, cleaning the bore of his M1907 'Colonial' rifle, wears Lebel belt equipment over a red flannel sash; note too the *gris-gris* amulet hanging round his neck for supernatural protection – this was tucked out of sight inside the jacket on formal occasions.

G: INDOCHINA

G1: *Caporal-fourrier*, Matas militia; Cochinchina, 1872

The Matas community were among the earliest to provide the French with local troops in South Vietnam, and ten years later they still formed an embodied militia divided into 'inspections'. They were described by Dr Morice as wearing a 'blue vest with yellow cuffs, marked on the left with the number of their inspection', a small woven hat with a small brass tip, under which the hair was tucked, and white trousers over bare feet. Our earlier figure is based on an evidently careful watercolour by Capt Bournissien de Valmont of the French Navy showing two Matas, the other figure being armed with a wavy-bladed polearm. The hat is shown as small and conical with a slight 'chimney' effect, covered with white cloth and secured with a red ribbon passing around the clubbed hair behind the neck to knot at the left. This type of headdress was made with narrow strips of bamboo and lined with tightly woven thin strips of reeds; its tip was crowned with a detachable brass 'pagoda' point, and it later received a brass frontal badge. Its shape allowed the soldier to shoot while lying flat on his front, which was not the case with European colonial helmets. The short, collarless, dark royal-blue jacket, worn open over an apparently black vest, is edged all around with red and has red pointed cuffs; a red waist sash is knotted at the left, over loose white trousers, short white gaiters and black shoes. The latter were almost a torture for Vietnamese feet, but some Matas, especially NCOs, nevertheless wore them as proudly as they did their badges of rank. The gold diagonal stripe on his upper sleeves identifies this man as a *caporal-fourrier* with administrative functions, and thus with some education – perhaps at the hands of the Christian missionaries who made many converts in Cochinchina. In 1862, about 20 per cent of the unit were armed with flintlock carbines and the others with Vietnamese polearms, which were also reported later by Dr Morice and Capt Valmont. This NCO has an M1840 percussion carbine with a *yatagan* bayonet, and carries ammunition in an M1845 *giberne* on the back of his belt. (*Le Tour du Monde*, 1875; Valmont Ms, Bibliothèque Nationale, Paris; Boisselier)

G2: *Soldat de 1ere classe, Tirailleurs Tonkinois*, 1884

The ten companies that existed before the formation of the first regiments were seen by Dr Hocquard in 1884 in the following dress: 'they wear a white linen blouse with red cuffs, blue trousers that come down only half down the calf, a conical-shaped hat painted with red, white and blue concentric circles. On their blouse, on the left side of the chest, is sewn a small piece of white cotton upon which their number is written in black. They are armed with the straight-bladed infantry [short] sabre and a rifle. They are bare-footed and bare-legged.' We reconstruct this man partly from a slightly later engraving, with a vest and trousers in the dark indigo blue characteristic of Tonkinese peasant clothing. The M1845 cartridge box is worn here at the front. Hocquard's 'sabre' is unidentifiable: we have given the Tirailleur the bayonet for the Chassepot M1866 Gendarmerie carbine that he carries. From the mid-1880s the Tirailleurs Tonkinois began receiving the same uniform as the Tirailleurs Annamites. (Engraving from photo in *Le Tour du Monde*, 1889; Boisselier)

G3: *Clairon, Régiment de Tirailleurs Annamites*; full dress, *c*.1902–14

In 1884, Dr Hocquard described the Tirailleurs Annamites as wearing 'a short blouse of black fabric that does not [entirely] cover their hips, long and wide trousers of the same colour, a red waist sash tied in a large knot in front and whose ends hang down to mid-thigh. They wear a round and flat hat in bamboo, covered by a layer of lacquer and garnished with brass ornaments [i.e. this true Annamese *salacco*]. Like all Annamites, they wear their hair long and put up in a little bun, which is fixed by a bone or wooden comb.' From about 1885 their uniform was dark blue; at some time during the 1880s a collar patch bearing the man's company number was added, but this was not continued. They initially wore sandals but were later also issued small-sized Army shoes. Each Tirailleur in Indochina was issued three jackets and trousers: dark blue with red trim for dress, white in summer, and plain black for campaign and fatigues, replaced with khaki from the mid-1890s.

This reconstruction of a bugler in full dress draws partly on Galot & Robert (1961). Photographs taken after 1900 still show Tirailleurs Tonkinois with a single M1877 'coffer' pouch, while the weapon is the M1902 *'fusil de Tirailleur Indochinois'* shortened to 3ft 8 inches. From 1830, all French Army buglers, drummers and trumpeters had diamond-pattern blue, white and red lace edging to the collar and cuffs, but the dimensions of the Indochinese *kéo* apparently did not allow the former. (*Le Tour du Monde*, 1889; Boisselier; Galot & Robert)

H: INDOCHINA

H1: Sergeant, *Linh Co* constabulary units, *c*.1892

As a distinction, Governor-General Lanessan assigned green ribbons to the *Linh Co* units in Tonkin and Annam, since this is traditionally the colour of hope. In November 1891, the government of Indochina ordered uniforms to be made for them annually in Hanoi: dark blue jackets of the same style as the Garde Civile, dark blue trousers, white jackets and trousers for summer (the colours sometimes being worn mixed, as here), green waist sashes instead of Garde Civile blue, and *salacco* hats trimmed with green. The bandana worn around the knotted hair was black, though one of Tran Van Minh's Garde Civile paintings shows dark brown, which was traditional for clothing in the Red River Delta of Tonkin. The gold lace sleeve chevron in the mounted troops' style identified sergeants, and junior ranks wore red chevrons. *Linh Co* units were usually armed with the M1874 Gras in its Gendarmerie carbine version, which took the Chassepot bayonet. (Circular, 16 November 1891, *Bulletin officiel de l'indochine française*, 1891)

H2: Civil Guard, *Garde Civile Indigène de l'Annam et du Tonkin*; field dress, *c*.1900

The dress uniform resembled that of the Tirailleurs (see illustrations on page 35): Vietnamese-style dark blue jacket and trousers, but with medium-blue hat ribbons on the *salacco* and matching sash and puttees. For field service they were issued from 1896 this khaki version. This man has an M1874 Gras rifle, one M1877 cartridge box, and one of several recorded variations on the home-made 'de Négrier' chest rig for extra packets. His kit is completed with a *musette* and a blanket roll; none of Tran Van Minh's paintings shows an issue canteen. (Watercolour by Tran Van Minh, Anne S. K. Brown Military Collection; *Recueil de la législation*)

H3: Private, *Tirailleurs Cambodgiens*; summer full dress, *c*.1905

The Tirailleurs Cambodgiens, raised from 1902, wore a Tirailleurs Annamites-style dark blue *kéo* blouse with brass buttons and red trim on the collar and pointed cuffs, matching trousers with red piping, white under-breeches and brown leather sandals. The headgear was a large Chasseurs Alpin'-style red beret, or a straw hat with a red band. In hot weather, this dress uniform was white in the Naval Troops' 1895 style and with the same anchor collar patches, a red sash and red puttees. The weapon is the M1902 *'fusil de Tirailleur Indochinois'*. (Vinkhuizen collection, NY Public Library; Boisselier)

INDEX

Note: figures in bold refer to illustrations.